ON DISTANT SHORE

Part 2

Sept. 7, 2016 – Feb. 2, 2017
In descending order

Val G. Abelgas

Published and printed

by TATAY JOBO ELIZES.
Self-Publisher
in 2017, under the
permission and authorization
of VAL G. ABELGAS,

ISBN - 13: 978 - 1976273667
ISBN - 10: 1976273668

Contact: job_elizes@yahoo.com
Website: http://tinyurl.com/mj76ccq

Special Note

Articles are arranged in reversed chronology descending from newer dates to older dates

About the author

VAL G. ABELGAS

Publisher-Editor, Philippine Post

Editor, www.thepinoyweekly.com

Columnist, On Distant Shore

valabelgas@aol.com

Val G. Abelgas, Publisher and Editor-in-Chief of the Los Angeles-based Philippine Post, has been a professional journalist for almost 45 years, 20 of them in Manila and 25 years in Los Angeles.

Val started as a sportswriter in the now defunct Philippine Daily Express in 1972 while still in his junior year in journalism at the University of the Philippines' Institute of Mass Communications. He rose to become city editor of then the country's biggest daily newspaper at a very young age of 24. He was the last managing editor of the Daily Express, which was closed down by the Cory Aquino administration in 1987. The next day, he moved to the Manila Standard as its first managing editor.

After stints as editorial consultant of the Philippine Star Group and later managing editor of the Philippine Times Journal, he and his family immigrated in 1991 to the United States, where he later obtained his green card as an alien of extraordinary ability in the field of journalism. In his first year in the US, he was editor of the Los Angeles Monitor and the next year became the first editor-in-chief of Balita. He moved to the Philippine Times in 1993, during which time he won the Newspaper of the Year and Columnist of the Year awards of the Philippine Press Club of America for two straight years in 1993 and 1994. In November 1993, he organized the first-ever nationwide convention of Filipino-American editors in Los Angeles with President Fidel V. Ramos as guest speaker. In 1995, he left the Philippine Times to join his wife Marisse in editing the Philippine Post and later became editor of Ang Peryodiko, the Pinoy Weekly and the Philippine Tribune. He published and edited two magazines with his wife, the Philippine Post Magazine and the Hiyas Magazine.

Before becoming a professional journalist, Abelgas was editor-in-chief of The Nucleus, official organ of the Manila Science High School, assistant news editor of the Philippine Collegian, official newspaper of the University of the Philippines, and editor-in-chief of the Campus Journal, laboratory newspaper of the UP-IMC.

Abelgas wrote a column, "As We See It," for the Philippines Daily Express in the 1980s. In 1992, he started writing his weekly "On Distant Shore" column, which is being published in 9 Filipino publications in the US and Canada.

Val has won numerous journalism awards both as a professional and campus journalist and served as director of the National Press Club of the Philippines five times and president of the Philippine Press Club of America. In 2016, he was named Journalist of the Year by the Filipino-American Press Club of California. He has travelled to more than 30 countries in official assignments as a journalist.

ooooo

Contents

1

An action guided by bigotry and injustice

February 2, 2017

DESCRIBED by the great President Abraham Lincoln as "a nation conceived in Liberty, and dedicated to the proposition that all men are created equal," the United States of America is now being transformed by one man into a nation guided by bigotry and injustice.

In just one week, the image crafted by the country's fathers and strengthened by 44 presidents before him is being irreparably damaged by a few strokes of the pen by a man who campaigned and marched to the White House on a message of hate and divisiveness.

On his very first day in office, US President Donald Trump started moves to isolate America from the rest of the world, announcing plans to build a $15-billion border wall and insisting neighbor Mexico pay for it. He also started burning bridges across the globe with plans to pull the United States out of the Trans-Pacific Partnership trade agreement that the US had initiated, and to renegotiate the North America Free Trade Agreement (NAFTA) with neighbors Mexico and Canada.

Earlier, Trump had hinted of plans to pull the US out of the North Atlantic Treaty Organization (NATO), which he called "obsolete," sending shock waves through the country's European allies.

On Friday, Trump signed an executive order indefinitely suspending the resettlement of Syrian refugees and temporarily banning people from seven predominantly Muslim nations from entering the United States. Because the order was made to take effect immediately without clear implementing guidelines, it created chaos in airports all over the US.

US immigration authorities began turning away or detaining travelers whose passports and records showed the remotest ties to the seven countries, including those already with valid travel visas. Even "green card" holders were held for hours or barred from returning to their families.

Outside airports and in other key places, demonstrators from all races and religious denominations marched in protest of the bigoted order. Immediately, five federal judges ordered a stop to parts of the executive action while 15 state attorneys general jointly condemned Trump's order.

California's Attorney General Xavier Becerra, in joining the 14 other attorneys general, said: "Justice in America doesn't live or die on the stroke of one man's pen regardless of how high his office. The Trump Administration's anti-religion, anti-refugee executive order is in so many ways unjust and anti-American. It discriminates against human beings based on their faith. It denies entry to those with proven and legitimate fears of death and persecution. It tramples on centuries of American tradition. The

Trump executive order should not stand and must be confronted as a constitutional overreach."

Blinded by his extreme bigotry, Trump has completely ignored the important role of immigrants in the US, seeing them only as terrorists, rapists, and criminals. I doubt if none of his many businesses has Mexican or Muslim immigrants, who in their own way have contributed largely to the success of his business operations.

Even high-tech companies, such as Google, Facebook, Microsoft, Apple, Uber, Netflix and Twitter, which generate billions more of dollars in revenues than his hotels and casinos, acknowledged the important role of immigrants in the growth of their companies and the US. The billionaire CEOs of these companies issued separate statements condemning Trump's immigration executive actions.

"Apple would not exist without immigration, let alone thrive and innovate the way we do. I've heard from many of you who are deeply concerned about the executive order issued yesterday restricting immigration from seven Muslim-majority countries. I share your concerns. It is not a policy we support," wrote Apple CEO Tim Cook.

For centuries, America has welcomed immigrants from all over the world, "the huddled masses yearning to breathe free," and with just one stroke of the pen, Trump virtually closed America's doors to a specific group of people. Lady Liberty must be shaking on her pedestal.

The order says, "The United States must ensure that those admitted to this country do not bear hostile attitudes toward it and its founding principles," and although it did not mention the word Muslim, by imposing the ban on seven countries with Muslim majorities, it clearly targeted Muslims, making it appear that all Muslims are a threat to the country's security. Ironically, while the order said it was being done to protect the country and its founding principles, discriminating against Muslims and of the nationals of the seven countries run counter to the founding father's principles of liberty and equality.

And while Trump and his allies justify the immigration action as a step to ensure homeland security, experts are concerned that it could instead pose extreme danger to the country. They said extremist groups can use it as a propaganda tool to boost their claim that America is not just targeting terrorists but is actually declaring war against Islam and Muslims all over the world.

The security experts are concerned that the executive action would make it easier for these groups to recruit or encourage young Muslims angered by Trump's bigoted action, including those already in the US, to take revenge against America.

Even Trump's Defense Secretary Jim Mattis warned of a ban against Muslims during the campaign, when the then Republican nominee was raising his rhetoric against Muslims. Mattis said: "This kind of thing is causing us great damage right now, and it's sending shock waves through this international system."

Trump is sending America to isolation from the rest of the world. In these times when the world has become a global village, America cannot afford what former President Barack Obama described as Trump's "naked self-interest and zero-sum diplomacy."

Ooooo

2
Let the journalists do their job
January 24, 3017

FILIPINOS in America are in a unique situation where in a span of six months, they are faced with having to contend with two of the most controversial and contentious national leaders to emerge in recent history, both in the homeland and in their adopted land. Having had to face uncertainty in their homeland with the vague domestic and foreign policies of tough-talking Philippine President Rodrigo Duterte and his equally chaotic Cabinet, Filipinos in the United States now face an even deeper sense of confusion and concern right on the very first day in office of US President Donald Trump.

At least, Duterte drew applause from many people, including this writer, for his inaugural address and demeanor, which many described as "precise, presidential and purposeful." He did not make any curse or threat, and went through his presidential agenda in a straight-forward manner and with a sense of clarity. He did not move away from his prepared speech.

What happened after that day is something else. He went back to diverting from his prepared speech, started cursing and making threats again, and making confusing statements that were obviously not consulted with his advisers and made many ask: Where is this country headed?

And each time his remarks drew protests and controversy, he blamed the media for inaccurate and irresponsible reporting.

His frequent feud with the media makes his similarities with his newfound friend Trump even more striking.

Deviating from the usual tone of inaugural addresses that calls for unity after a long and divisive elections, Trump chose to proceed as if he were still on the campaign trail and lambasted the Washington politicians gathered behind him, including Republicans who reluctantly supported him, in a manner that demagogues have historically done before him with populist and ultra-nationalist rhetoric.

He was obviously addressing his avid supporters and not the entire Americans, the majority of whom elected somebody else but had to vow to the rules of the electoral voting system. With millions of Americans and millions more around the globe awaiting how he would make America great again, as he had repeatedly avowed during the campaign, Trump instead launched his usual campaign rhetoric that roused his supporters but dampened the hopes of majority of Americans.

And millions of Americans were left asking: Where is this country headed?

The morning after the inaugural – Trump's first official day in office — millions of these Americans marched in several cities all over America, supported by smaller protest rallies all over the world, to vent their anger on Trump whom they described as racist, fascist, sexist, and a few other unsavory words.

But instead of addressing the protesters to allay their fears and soothe their anger, Trump chose to spend his first day in office to launch a bitter attack on news media. He falsely accused journalists of creating a rift between him and intelligence agencies and of deliberately understating the size of the crowd that attended his inauguration. He called journalists "among the most dishonest human beings on earth."

Later in the day, he sent his press secretary to scold members of the press and warn them that the government would hold them accountable for false reporting. In his very first press briefing in the White House, Press Secretary Sean Spicer said news organizations had deliberately misstated the size of the inaugural crowd in an attempt to sow divisions at a time when Trump was trying to unify the country, warning that the new administration would hold them to account.

Earlier, Trump also angered some officials of the Central Intelligence Agency, where he went on Saturday to make peace with the intelligence community because instead of paying tribute to the sacrifices of members of the intelligence community who died in the line of duty, the

President used the occasion mostly to attack the press.

Trump complained that the news media used photographs of "an empty field" to make it seem as if his inauguration did not draw many people.

"We caught them in a beauty," Trump said of the news media, "and I think they're going to pay a big price." Spicer later claimed that Trump had drawn "the largest audience to ever witness an inauguration," a statement that photographs and live TV showed to be false.

Two contrasting photos posted by a New York Times reporter on Tweet clearly showed the Obama inauguration in 2009 drawing a much larger crowd than Trump's. Spicer also claimed that the number of riders in Washington-area transit clearly showed that more people came to witness Trump's inauguration than Obama's in 2099. But transit authority figures showed there were 782,000 riders that year, compared with 571,000 riders this year.

In other words, while Trump and his press secretary were accusing the news media of false reporting, they were actually the ones who made false claims about the inaugural crowd.

Trump said he is, in his own words, in a "running war" with the media, a war he is not expected to win just as Duterte is not expected to win his own war with the Philippine news media.

Trump should have realized by now that a strong, truthful and vigilant media is one of the major reasons America has become the bastion of democracy. Duterte, on the other hand, should have known by now that nearly all his predecessors waged their own war against media and lost. Former President Joseph Estrada, for example, tried to muzzle the critical Philippine Daily Inquirer by asking major advertisers to boycott the newspaper. Several months later, Estrada was ousted by People Power.

Only one Philippine president won a battle against the press. The late dictator Ferdinand Marcos padlocked newspaper offices and TV and radio stations when he declared martial law in 1972, but while he won the battle, he eventually lost the war when the so-called mosquito press started stinging him in the 80s. He was ousted in the first People Power in 1986.

Government leaders should stop blaming and warring on media, and focus instead on wars that they should fight – against corruption, poverty and other ills that afflict society. Let the journalists do their job of reporting the truth to build an informed citizenry.

Ooooo

3
The poor had been had again
January 10, 2017

MILLIONS of Filipinos are beginning to realize that they have been taken for a ride again by politicians who make promises that they either did not really intend to fulfill or they did not even weigh if doable or not. We are a hopelessly hopeful and trustful people that many of us take these promises as basis for electing their leaders.

For instance, then Davao City Mayor Rodrigo Duterte vowed during the campaign that he would rid the country of drug pushers and users in six months even if he was told that eliminating 3.4 million drug pushers and users and completely eradicating the country's illegal drug trade would be impossible to do even in one or perhaps, even his entire six-year term.

But millions, who were understandably frustrated by the nagging problem, believed him and elected him to the presidency. Now, the brutal drug war has become a growing nightmare that has only fueled a culture of death and impunity in the country. Worse, it has divided the people into those who didn't care about human life and the rule of law, and those who still give value to compassion and justice.

Another major promise that was bound to be broken was that he would rid the country of corruption. In the very first general appropriations act – a whopping P3.35-billion budget — that he signed as president, the much-maligned and illegal graft-ridden pork barrel system remained, albeit in a more hideous form, as revealed by Sen. Ping Lacson.

"Change is coming? Maybe, but it's pork allocations changing hands from the Liberal Party congressmen [under the previous administration] to those from Mindanao," Lacson said sarcastically in a statement to the media.

"To put a veil on their post-enactment participation, in connivance with those in the executive branch, the legislators now identify their projects prior to submission of the budget to Congress, during the budget deliberations and even during the bicameral conference," Lacson said in an interview.

Still wondering why despite having only three elected congressmen from his party and one in the Senate, Duterte is tightly in control of both chambers of Congress? Duterte, a long-time politician raised in a political family, is not naïve to not know that to control Congress, he should have the resources or the "grease from the pork" to make our honorable congressmen and senators toe the line. Voters are the ones who were too naïve to believe blindly a promise made during a political campaign.

Duterte made several other promises that some supporters are beginning to realize was just that, a campaign promise. But this one would hit them directly and is certain to trigger much louder protests – the promise to increase the meager SSS pensions as early as this month.

Millions of SSS pensioners, many of them receiving a measly P1,200 a month in retirement pension, were looking forward to a happy new year with a promised increase of P2,000 a month starting this month.

During his first press conference as president-elect in May in Davao City, Duterte said the Social Security System (SSS) pension is in place precisely for employees to save up to their elderly years when the time comes for them to retire. He said the current amount of pension at P1,200 is not enough for the elderly to afford their medical needs.

Duterte even castigated his predecessor, President Benigno S. Aquino III, for vetoing the bill that would grant pensioners an across-the-board increase of P2,000 a month. Aquino had said that granting the increase without a corresponding hike in members' contribution would render the SSS bankrupt by 2029.

"Tama pala si Aquino," Duterte seemed to say when he expressed the same concerns raised by Aquino, which is the same reason raised by Duterte's economic managers in advising the President to reject the proposal.

The militants rightfully protested at once.

"Change has come, they say, and yet Duterte and neoliberal-minded economic advisers are repeating exactly the same flawed justification made by former President Noynoy Aquino to veto the SSS pension hike," said Anakbayan chairperson Vencer Crisostomo.

Budget Secretary Benjamin Diokno said Duterte could not keep the promise to increase the SSS pension by P2,000 now that he is President. Diokno was basically admitting that Duterte the President is different from Duterte the candidate. So, is he admitting that the 16 million who voted for him were shortchanged?

Duterte promised to look for a win-win solution to the SSS pension increase dilemma. The Duterte economic managers are saying the SSS pension increase is only possible if the members' contributions or premiums are correspondingly raised.

Pensioners and militants are saying the pension hike is possible without increasing contributions by taking aggressive legal steps to collect over P367 million in premiums and penalties from 139 delinquent corporations and employers that have been remiss in their responsibility under the SSS law and by stopping payment of millions of pesos in bonuses to SSS officials and commission members every Christmas season.

Others are saying that the SSS needs to hire investment experts to make sure the agency is making wise investments with the members' money.

Pension experts, including former SSS executive vice president Horacio Templo, who now writes a column for the Manila Standard, believe all of the above are needed to enable the SSS to increase pensions while ensuring the stability of the pension agency.

So why not grab the bull by the horn and implement all these proposed actions, including increasing the members' contributions, to address once and for all the need to increase the monthly pensions of retirees, who obviously cannot get by with the minimum P1,200 monthly pension, instead of promising to raise it every election and not being able to do it?

The same Duterte economic managers – Diokno, Finance Secretary Sonny Dominguez and Economic Planning Secretary Ernesto Pernia – have been blamed for many of Duterte's failed promises, including the promised two-year ban on land conversions and the ban on "endo" or contractualization, among others.

Duterte promised so many pro-people actions and yet appointed neo-liberals and capitalists to important Cabinet positions, and now the millions who voted for him are realizing presidential candidates would promise even the heavens to get their votes.

The poor had been had again.

Ooooo

4
A year of hope and uncertainty
January 3, 2017

A FEELING of uncertainty has deepened in the Philippines as coup rumors and martial law talk ushered in the New Year. Both talks about the possibility of destabilization moves and a coup attempt and speculations about the possible declaration of martial law were started by President Duterte himself and his allies.

As early as two months ago, the tough-talking President accused the Liberal Party of plotting to oust him and allow Vice President Leni Robredo to take over as president. Of course, leaders of the Liberal Party, including Robredo, vehemently denied such a plot and warned that Duterte may be setting the stage for the declaration of martial law.

Communications Secretary Martin Andanar later revealed plots by some Filipino community leaders to destabilize the Duterte administration through massive demonstrations in 2017 and to instigate the military to launch a coup against him.

Duterte later warned these Filipino-Americans, ostensibly led by the widow of wealthy black businessman, that such moves would not be tolerated. Businesswoman Loida Nicolas Lewis, obviously the wealthy woman identified by Duterte, denied such a plot, saying that "the President was being given misinformation designed to divide the country and advance the interests of a certain political group while casting Filipino Americans in an unfavorable light".

And then just four days before the onset of the new year, Manila Times publisher Dante A. Ang, a public relations adviser of former President Gloria Macapagal Arroyo, wrote a news story datelined Lisbon, Portugal that revealed an alleged document wherein former US Ambassador to the Philippines Philip Goldberg supposedly recommended actions that would destabilize and ultimately remove Duterte from office.

The US State Department denied the existence of the alleged Goldberg document, but it triggered rumors of an impending coup against the Duterte administration.

There can only be two reasons why the Duterte camp has been insisting that the opposition and other groups are plotting destabilization moves and coup attempt. Either this administration is too insecure about its ability to stay in power for six years, or it is setting the stage for its own coup from within – a declaration of martial law in the coming months.

Opposition leaders, particularly Robredo, and Senators Leila de Lima and Antonio Trillanes IV, have been warning about a possible declaration of martial law by Duterte. The President cannot blame the opposition and other groups for such speculation considering that Duterte himself has been insinuating that he would declare a revolutionary government, if necessary, to ensure the changes that he wanted in the country.

Even while campaigning, Duterte said he would abolish Congress and form a revolutionary government if the Legislative and Judicial branches of government blocked his reforms. He said a revolutionary government was necessary because the current Constitution can no longer address the many problems besetting the country.

Trillanes warned then: "The moment he tries to declare a revolutionary government, that is also going to be the day he will be removed from office. This guy has no respect for democratic institutions."

In August, Duterte threatened to declare martial law if Chief Justice Ma. Lourdes Sereno would continue to block his war against drugs. This was the time when Sereno questioned the police's arrests without warrant.

After Duterte declared a state of national emergency in early September, presidential legal adviser Salvador Panelo said his office is toying with the idea of giving Duterte expanded powers under a "constitutional dictatorship," wherein the President would have powers over both the executive and legislative branches to speed up reforms.

Duterte had insisted that he would not declare martial law, but the idea advanced by Panelo, one of his closest advisers, seemed to show otherwise. Duterte would repeatedly deny any plans to declare martial law.

But just three days before Christmas Day, Duterte seemed to contradict himself again when he said that he wanted to amend the provisions of the 1987 Constitution that check a president's power to declare and implement martial law. He noted that he could not proceed on declaring martial law as such authority is subject to review by both Congress and the Supreme Court.

These provisions were included in the 1987 Constitution precisely to prevent the Chief Executive from abusing the power to declare martial law and to prevent a repeat of the country's experience under the late dictator President Ferdinand E. Marcos, whose greatest fan is Duterte himself.

Remember that Marcos repeatedly denied he would declare martial law after successively declaring a state of lawlessness and suspending the writ of habeas corpus prior to declaring martial law a few months later in 1972.

"This is ridiculous," Marcos said then. "Who would want to declare martial law?"

Here's what Duterte said in November when concerns were raised about the possibility of his suspending the writ of habeas corpus and ultimately declaring martial law: "I am not a fan of Martial Law. I am a lawyer. People are afraid of

Martial Law but if ever, Martial Law is a contingency to meet widespread violence."

Duterte said he was a lawyer as if to insinuate that he had respect for the rule of law, but so was Marcos, an even better lawyer who topped the Bar even while under detention for the murder of his father's political rival Julio Nalundasan.

A few days before declaring martial law, Marcos announced that the communists were now using "sex, pornography and drugs, among other techniques," to destroy the moral fiber of the youth." Sounds familiar, except that instead of the communists, Duterte is now talking of how drug syndicates are destroying the nation's moral fiber.

And so the people enter the new year with new hopes, but also with renewed concerns about turbulent times ahead as rumors of an impending coup or martial law pervades the political atmosphere.

Whether or not either a coup or martial law happens this year or in the coming years, we must keep our vigilance so that a repeat of dictatorial rule does not happen again to our beloved country.

Ooooo

5
A happy and hopeful people
January 1, 2017

IT shouldn't surprise us anymore that every year, Filipinos are ranked among the happiest people in the world and are ever hopeful that the coming year would be better than the previous one. Despite the poverty around them, and the endless disasters and tragedies that wreak havoc in their lives year in and year out, the Filipinos remain among the happiest and most optimistic people in the world.

Nearly every year, a Gallup worldwide survey shows that the Filipinos are in the top 10 happiest people on earth, while surveys by both Pulse Asia and the Social Weather Station consistently show that more than 90% of Filipinos are optimistic that the coming year would be better than the previous one.

The annual Gallup poll asks about 1,000 people in each of 148 countries if in the past year, they were well-rested, had been treated with respect, smiled or laughed a lot, learned or did something interesting and felt feelings of enjoyment the previous day.

The pollsters note that people from "prosperous nations can be deeply unhappy ones, and poverty-stricken ones are often awash in positivity, or at least a close approximation of it."

I had often wondered why despite the economic difficulties and day-to-day problems being experienced by the Philippines, Filipinos still seem to be a happy lot — always laughing and smiling, never running out of jokes, and always partying.

Everyone knows that a big majority of Filipinos are below the poverty level, and yet every Tomas, Ricardo and Pedro owns a cell phone. Try walking through Metro Manila and, most probably, every other Filipino you come across has a cell phone glued to his ear — the businessman, the junior executive, the clerical employee, the jeepney driver, the security guard, the student, and yes, even the meat vendor in your favorite market.

They say Filipinos could hardly make both ends meet, and yet every other Filipino male seems to be in the beerhouse and night clubs almost every night, gobbling up beer and liquor till their big tummies could take it no more, and spending money on very young women known as guest relations officers (GROs).

They say inflation rate is high, and yet the malls are always full. Filipinos never seem to tire shopping. While Americans tend to do their shopping on weekends or during holidays, Filipinos do theirs any time of the day, any day of the week, sale or no sale.

They say many Filipinos are forever trapped in minimum wage, and yet you will hardly see Filipinos who are not dressed in the latest fashion, from the high-priced Nike shoes, to fancy Guess watches, and Tommy Hilfiger or Polo by Ralph Lauren shirts. Of course, again, you can't figure out which ones are genuine, and which ones are imitation ones.

They say many Filipinos eat mostly tuyo and daing, and yet look at the fast food chains and plush restaurants — from McDonald's to Mang Donald's, from Pinausukan Restaurant to pinausukan (mobile eateries exposed to jeepneys' exhaust, usually at jeep terminals), from Bughaw Restaurant to bughaw eateries (bughaw nang bughaw ng langaw) — they are always full to capacity.

They say Filipinos are so poor, and yet all the entertainment joints are full — the cinemas, the disco joints, the beer houses, the massage parlors, the restaurants, the dancing halls (for ballroom dancing), the hotel lobbies, the motels, the casinos, the billiard halls, the inuman sa tindahan sa kanto, the cockpits, the race tracks, the basketball arenas, the concerts, the karaoke bars, etc.

They say Filipinos can hardly afford the basic necessities, and yet look at the number of Mercedes Benzes, BMWs, Hondas, Toyotas, Mitsubishis, Jeeps, Explorers, Pajeros, and other new cars that compete for little road space with run-down jeepneys and 20-year-old or even 30-year-old cars.

They say life is so difficult in the Philippines, and yet the golf courses and tennis courts are full even on weekdays. And Filipino golfers have the latest in golf equipment, and wear the most expensive golf clothing and footwear. And where else can you find a golfer whose bag is carried by a caddy and whose head is protected by sexy umbrella girls as he trots around the golf course?

How can the Philippines be so poor, and the Filipinos so extravagant? Or is it because the Filipinos are so extravagant, that's why the Philippines is so poor?

The answer, I presume, goes back to the influence of the Spaniards, who reigned supreme over the Philippines for more than 400 years. Look at the Mexicans and other Latinos, they also tend to be fashionable, love to party, and love to have fun, although they can hardly afford it. And among the top 10 happiest people in the world according to Gallup, eight are from Latin America.

Was it President Manuel L. Quezon who called this ability of the Filipinos to adjust to life's difficulties as "the resiliency of Filipinos"? Resilient as a bamboo, he said, meaning Filipinos have the ability to bend with the wind, just like the bamboo, and not be uprooted by it.

"Mahirap na nga ang buhay, magmumukmok pa tayo?" a Filipino would justify his tendency to have fun despite the hard times. "Bakit ipapahalata pa nating mahirap tayo?" another would say.

Filipinos generally love to show off. Many Filipinos would wear the latest in fashion when he goes out, but once inside the house, wears old puruntong shorts and dirty shirts that have seen better days. He would spend a big chunk of his paycheck to pay monthly installments on a Honda Civic, but lives in a cramped, old apartment with worn-down furniture, while he feeds his family with tuyo, salmon or sardinas.

Is this trait good or bad?

If you look at it from the economic perspective, it's not good. Because of the Filipinos' too much love for fun, they become unproductive. Instead of working devotedly during office hours, many employees spend two to three hours outside of the office ostensibly for lunch. Many executives play golf or play footsie with their queridas, instead of overseeing the operations of their businesses. Because they spend too much time in the evenings in beerhouses and other entertainment joints, they tend to be sloppy in their work the next day. Because of their uncontrolled spending, inflation rate continues to soar. And because of the lopsided spending on entertainment, there is hardly anything left for savings or investments, such as retirement funds and college education, or for home purchases.

From the social perspective, it's not really that bad. Because of their ability to have fun despite the difficulties, Filipinos are able to smile genuine smiles, and laugh genuine laughs even during the most critical and most difficult periods in their lives. Uprisings and revolutions will never succeed in the Philippines because Filipinos are able to ease their tensions, and laugh away their troubles. It is not accidental that Filipinos make fun out of even the most tragic episodes in their lives.

So, Filipinos all over the world, don't worry too much about our kababayans back home, because they will be the first to tell you: "Don't worry, be happy!"

Ooooo

6
A distant Christmas
December 23, 2016

FOR Filipinos who have been outside of the Philippines for years, Christmas is both a time for rejoicing and a time for remembering. Even as the Filipino in America begins to feel the holiday mood immediately after Thanksgiving when people start shopping for gifts and Christmas decors, he feels at the same time a longing for home. For nothing beats Christmas in the Philippines!

After living on a distant shore all these years, I can truly say that nothing beats the way Filipinos celebrate Christmas. The genuine joy that the season brings to millions of Filipinos in the Philippines is the same reason why the hundreds of thousands of Filipinos living outside the Philippines yearn for home at this time of the year.

For even just during those few days that Christmas is celebrated in the Philippines, many Filipinos feel they can share the blessings that the world brings. Because of the mandatory 13th month pay and the bonuses paid by nearly all companies, big and small alike, many people are able to afford what they can only dream about the rest of the year.

For the children of the poor, the Christmas season is only one of two instances when their parents can afford to buy them new set of clothes and new pairs of shoes, the other being the school opening. Christmas is also the only time for many of these children to own a brand new toy, often as a gift from their parents or from their ninong or ninang.

The Christmas season is also their chance to earn some money to buy candies or toys. As early as December, young boys and girls prepare their instruments for their traditional carolling, making drums out of empty cans covered by plastic, tambourine out of bottle caps, and even just a pair of sticks to provide percussion. At dusk, they form into groups of three or four, and make their rounds starting on the night of Dec. 16 until Christmas eve. At the end of each night, the carolers count their earnings and divide them equally among themselves.

While the kids look forward to the advent of dusk during those nine days to earn some money, the teenagers await with anticipation the coming of dawn during that same period. For these teenagers, it is a chance to be with their crushes, girlfriends or boyfriends as they walk to the church in the biting cold. As early as three in the morning, from Dec. 16 to Dec. 24, they wake up and wear their best sweaters or jackets, have fun with their barkadas on the way to church, only to sleep while the mass is going on.

After the mass, they bounce back to life to join their friends again, feast on bibingkas and puto bungbong on their way home, and hang around a bit before being called home by their parents.

Towards midnight on Christmas Eve, parents and their children don their Christmas clothes and trek back to church for the Midnight

Mass. The church becomes a venue for both solemn celebration of Christmas and a chance to mingle with friends again.

From the church, families retreat to their homes for the traditional noche buena, a minor preview of the grand celebration at lunchtime the next day. The noche buena often consists of pan amerikano (bread loaf) or pan de sal, keso (queso de bola for those who can afford), hot dog, coffee or hot chocolate, etc. Noche buenas are usually only for the family.

But the grand Christmas celebration, usually at midday of Christmas Day, is for the entire clan. It is an occasion for children and grandchildren to gather together in the house of the patriarch or matriarch of the clan. Family members exchange gifts, catch up on each other's lives, and partake of the sumptuous meal. Children play games, the male family members drink beer or liquor, everybody participates in a singing session (using karaoke or otherwise), and the female members engage in endless banter.

Towards the afternoon, children, accompanied by their parents, visit their ninong and ninang to get their Christmas presents. Others visit friends, watch movies, and drink with friends. The merrymaking goes on till late at night. But the fun does not end there, because in six days, everybody gears up for a noisy New Year's Eve revelry.

At least once a year, during the Christmas season, Filipinos are able to let off steam from the pressures of trying to survive, the poor are able to enjoy a bit of material happiness, families renew their bonds, and everyone has fun.

Christmas brings pure and genuine happiness to many Filipinos. It is this kind of joy that a Filipino living in a foreign land misses sorely about Christmas. It is this kind of Christmas celebration that Filipinos living on distant shores can only reminisce about.

Ooooo

7
Impunity and the rule of law
December 12, 2016

BE careful what you wish for.

When Filipinos wished their next president would be a strong leader, one who would not be afraid to strictly enforce the law even if it goes against those wielding wealth and power, they did not envision a despotic leader who would ignore the rule of law, and enforce his will even if it violates the law.

Now, we have in our midst a leader who does not only have a penchant to disrespect the rule of law, but one who threatens anyone that blocks his way as he pursues his one-track quest to rid the country of illegal drugs and anyone who peddles or uses them. More than 6,000 bodies lay on the wayside less than six months since President Duterte became leader of the more than 100 million Filipinos and he vows to relentlessly pursue his brutal drug war until the last drug user or peddler has been removed from the streets.

He has launched personal battles with those who dared criticize his method of cleansing the country of criminals and drug addicts, including endless tirades against leaders of the free world – the United States, the United Nations, the European Union, Australia and so many others, calling them "hypocrites" and "sons of whore" and warning to cut ties with them.

He threatened to demolish his biggest local critic – Sen. Leila de Lima – that gave his loyal lackeys in the House of Representatives the go-signal to launch the biggest demolition job ever in that House of Honorables. To her credit, De Lima has fought back valiantly where others may have folded silently.

Even before he officially became President of the Philippines, Duterte had already threatened media by saying that media members are fair game for assassinations if they were corrupt, which perhaps explain why some publications and broadcast media have become tame and meek amidst the daily murders happening in the country.

And then he threatened police, judges and local officials nationwide by claiming he has a list of people engaged in "narco-politics" and that he wouldn't hesitate to include them in his brutal campaign. In no time, officials who learned they were on the list surrendered to authorities to deny such accusations, but some of them ended up dead anyway after allegedly fighting it out with lawmen. Those who were not in the list dare not cross his path.

The Supreme Court protested the inclusion of judges in the list and Chief Justice Sereno ordered judges not to issue warrants unless they are within the bounds of the law, but which judge would dare defy the police who have been virtually given blanket authority by the President in his war against illegal drugs by saying he would protect policemen and even reward them if they killed suspected drug users and pushers?

Recently, Duterte also threatened to include lawyers of suspected drug lords in the war against drugs, which completes his trampling of the rule of law and the basic rights provided by the Constitution, which gives suspects the right to be deemed innocent until proven guilty, to have a fair trial, and to have legal representation.

While we understand Duterte's frustration with the slow grind of the wheels of justice, the three branches of government – the Executive, Legislative and Judiciary – should sit down and find ways to get the wheels moving faster and not scrap the suspects' rights altogether just because those tasked to render justice have been negligent in their duties.

But the most troubling sign that the rule of law has no place in this administration is when Duterte categorically stated during an event commemorating the UN Convention of Corruption last week that despite the findings of the Department of Justice and the National Bureau of Investigation that the killing of Mayor Roland Espinosa and another detainee inside a Leyte prison by elements of the Criminal Investigation and Detection Group (CIDG) was a "rubout," Duterte said he stood by the CIDG's claim that they killed Espinosa after the latter shot it out with them while they were serving a search warrant in the dead of night.

"I will not allow these guys to go to prison. I don't care if the NBI says it was murder. Anyway, the NBI and the Department of Justice (DOJ) are both under [my authority]," Duterte said during a speech last week, referring to the CIDG operatives.

"I will be the one to answer for it and go to prison. I have no problem with that. When I was young, I went in and out of prison. I'm used to it," he said. He added: "For us mayors, who will we believe? The policemen or [the] criminals? If the police said that's really the truth, but the NBI said it was murder, what the police told me is the truth for me."

His statement was a clear rejection of the findings of the NBI and the DOJ, which recommended the filing of murder charges against them CIDG men. In his arrogance, Duterte wouldn't even allow criminal proceedings to go through the normal processes. Even if the case goes to court, there is always the statement of the President no less hanging over the heads of the NBI, the prosecutors and the judge. Would they dare embarrass the President?

De Lima hinted that the President could be impeached for his statement, to which Duterte replied with his usual arrogant line: "They can go ahead. Maraming daldal (They talk too much). I have to satisfy their lust for whatever. Let them be. Impeachable? Go ahead."

This recent outbursts by the President in defense of policemen contribute immensely to the culture of impunity in the country. His stubborn defense of policemen involved in extrajudicial killings only embolden murderers to commit their criminal acts with heightened impunity.

During the campaign, Duterte promised that he would pardon policemen who kill criminals, or even civilians, in the line of duty. Also during the campaign in February, Duterte said he would provide a "pre-signed form" to law enforcers, which would assure the latter of presidential pardon should they get prison terms for deaths during encounters with criminals.

Candidate Duterte also said that if he got elected, he would direct policemen and the military to not be deterred in killing "all" criminals because it is his "personal order."

These statements obviously emboldened policemen and vigilantes to start shooting down suspects as soon as it was clear that Duterte would be president, assured that they would go unpunished.

What is even alarming is that Duterte has rejected all opposition to his brutal war on drugs and arrogantly declares that the killings would continue until the last drug user or pusher has been placed out of commission. By his own estimate, there are 3.4 million drug addicts and dealers in the country. Does that mean we are just seeing the beginning of a deep-seethed cleansing and that we should expect more bloodied bodies on our streets?

Impunity feeds on the breakdown of the rule of law.   Ooooo

8
Why punish poor for govt's inefficiency?
December 5, 2016

I JUST came from a brief trip to the Philippines with my wife to be with her mother on the latter's 89th birthday, and like most who have recently been to the homeland, the horrendous traffic marred an otherwise eventful visit. A trip from a western point in Manila and Quezon City to the Makati Financial District would take at least two hours almost at any given time, except perhaps very early in the morning or very late at night.

A happy surprise greets a visitor at the Ninoy Aquino International Airport, where despite its being tagged the fifth worst international airport in Asia has many better things to offer. For one, there seems just half of the crowd that used to hang around at the terminal – no porters who pressure you into letting them push the cart for you; no shady characters who offer their services for a fee, of course. You are let alone to get your own cart, which are a-plenty and for free and to wait for your baggage. The lines at the immigration section are not as long, officers are polite and look friendly and do not make hints of a "pasalubong" or "papasko."

At the customs section, I was surprised that they did not bother to ask what was in the baggage nor, again, hint at tips. They look at your passport and let you go. "Am I in Manila?" I asked myself. Wha, no "tanim-bala" or "laglag-droga"? No words like: "Sir, ang dami mong chocolates, baka pwedeng maambunan ng isa?" "Sir, magpapasko na, Merry Christmas, sir!"

In any case, it was a pleasant surprise and for that, we should thank President Rodrigo Duterte. Give credit where credit is due. Whether it was caused by fear or just strict implementation, it just goes to show that many positive things could be done in the Philippines if the national leadership would just fully and strictly implement existing laws.

But once outside the terminal, the nightmare begins. No, not because the shady characters had just moved outside where there are less enforcement. It's the horrible traffic right outside NAIA all the way to wherever you are going. Suddenly, you forget the happy experience you just had at the airport because traffic was almost at a standstill, far worse than I last visited three years ago.

And to top it all, motorists continue to be the same undisciplined, reckless drivers they have always been. And yet, you can't blame them because if you stayed on your lane throughout your trip, it would probably take you another 30 minutes or so of driving. Then, there is also the problem of motorcycles weaving through traffic like kamikaze drivers.

By the time you get to where you are staying, you'll be so tired from the two-hour traffic after squeezing yourself in that tiny Economy seat and trying to sleep sitting down for close to 16 hours, you'd want to postpone the niceties of family welcome till the next day, and just fall down and sleep!

Let me cite one example of the traffic situation. On a Tuesday, we decided to take a taxi at 6 a.m. from The Fort to Sampaloc, Manila. It took us just 30 minutes and P198 in fare. Going back around 3 p.m., using exactly the same route in my brother-in-law's car, it took us close to two-and-a-half hours! That means a trip that can be made in 30 minutes before heavy traffic sets in can take more than two hours longer in normal Metro traffic.

The obvious reason for the ever-growing traffic problem is that Metro Manila is too congested. With almost 13 million people living in an area of only 620 square kilometers, Metro Manila is the 9th most populous metropolitan area in Asia. But we all know that in recent years, the metropolitan region has basically expanded into the nearby erstwhile farm areas of Bulacan, Cavite, Laguna, Rizal and Batangas for a total population of more than 24 million, making it, according to Wikipedia, the fourth most populous urban area in the world!

While Metro Manila's population has doubled since 1980 and quadrupled if counting the extended provinces, the construction of roads and skyways, and the development of mass transportation system such as the MRT (Metro Rail Transit) and the LRT (Light Rail Transit) systems has lagged further behind, not helped by the fact that rampant corruption has derailed the systems literally and figuratively.

As the population painfully awaits the construction of more roads and skyways and the addition of more MRT and LRT routes and trains, the monstrous traffic jams in virtually all Metro Manila roads (yes, including small back roads and alleys), the number of cars and other vehicles crawling on Metro's narrow roads continues to increase exponentially.

Can the people afford to purchase cars? Normally, no. But car dealers and finance companies have made it much easier for even ordinary people to buy new or used cars.

All of my brothers and sisters, and many of their children, for example, now have cars. When before they rented jeepneys or mini-vans to attend the traditional family reunions whenever somebody from abroad arrives, they now arrived in different cars and could not find parking in the neighborhood because most of my brother's neighbors now have two cars each themselves.

Parking has also become a problem in many neighborhoods because of this situation, which also contributes in making minor roads more congested.

For as a low as a down payment of P15,000 to P30,000, one can buy a new or used car, without credit check and minimal requirement on monthly income. You can just imagine how many families would jump at such an offer! You can also imagine how many thousands of cars this liberal financing has added to the traffic jams and how many more it would add to the monstrosity of the situation!

While it takes just a sign of the pen to add cars to the streets, it would take years before those skyways being built all over the metropolis could even be finished and more trains and routes could be added to the mass transit systems. Go figure it out.

Finance Secretary Sonny Dominguez thinks he has a partial solution to the problem of expanding vehicle population. He wants to restructure the excise tax on automobiles not only to partly ensure the financial sustainability of the government's 10-point socio-economic agenda on inclusive growth, but also to help deal with the worsening traffic crisis in Metro Manila and other highly congested urban centers.

"What's the point of buying a new car and not moving in the streets? The point of the matter is we want to direct the people to go to public transport, and we are making big investments in public transport, particularly the bus rapid transit system, and we're fixing up the trains, whose maintenance has been neglected over the years," Dominguez said.

Dominguez said a highly progressive tax on automobiles will discourage the purchase of new cars, which, in turn, will help stop traffic congestion from getting worse, and reduce air pollution and the carbon footprint.

Makes sense, but will it discourage people from buying cars? The poor, maybe. To the rich, it doesn't matter. They'll still buy all the cars they want. They're driving away the poor from the streets to take the LRT and MRT trains that are packed like sardines, stink, and so ill-maintained one needs to take insurance before taking the sweaty, bumpy ride. Why punish the poor for government's inefficiency?

Why not fix the mass transport system first before depriving people of the privilege to buy their own cars? But Dominguez says the government needs the money to fix the mass transport system and to build more roads. It's a simple case of the chicken or the egg. What do you think?

Ooooo

9
Bastusang Pambansa
November 30, 2016

THEY CALL themselves "Honorable" and want to be addressed your honor at the end of every statement. And yet for seven agonizing hours, the congressmen at the hearing of the Committee on Justice showed the nation why bloggers have called their place of work the "Bastusang Pambansa" because that's what they did last Thursday – to embarrass the subject of all these hullabaloo, Senator Leila de Lima.

In aid of legislation, as they are wont to say, the committee members grilled De Lima's erstwhile bodyguard, driver and lover, Ronnie Dayan, asking questions that was so personal it didn't serve any purpose for any kind of legislation related to illegal drugs. Instead, the "honorable" lawmakers were obviously out to humiliate and persecute a lady senator whose only obvious mistake at this point was that she fell for a man in her employ, and worse, crossed the path of the sitting President.

It is not a secret that President Rodrigo Duterte explodes in anger each time somebody criticizes or questions his brutal drug war that has killed more than 4,000 mostly poor Filipinos. He was still mayor of Davao City when De Lima first earned Duterte's ire when the then chair of the Commission on Human Rights investigated the so-called Davao Death Squad that had been accused of hundreds of extrajudicial killings in the city.

And then in July, not yet warmed up to her Senate seat, De Lima stood several times to criticize the daily death of drug dealers and users and investigated the killings resulting from Duterte's drug war until she was ousted as chair of the Senate committee on justice. Her unceremonious ouster from the important chair was obviously just the beginning of a seething vengeance as Duterte's allies in the House of Representatives started linking her to the illegal drug trade in the National Bilibid Prison.

Unable to present solid evidence that would link her to illegal drug trade and send her to prison, the President's "honorable" lackeys seem to have decided they would destroy her person instead, launching a character assassination reminiscent of the destruction of then Supreme Court Chief Justice Renatpo Corona, also in the early years of the previous administration.

What else would you call the line of questioning by the congressmen that day? The "your honors" spent most of the seven hours not establishing beyond hearsay and more importantly, beyond reasonable doubt that De

Lima knowingly received drug money from suspected drug lord Kerwin Espinosa and some drug lords operating from inside the Bilibid, and that she used this money for her senatorial campaign.

Instead, they asked Dayan very private and personal questions about his relationship with De Lima when the senator herself had already admitted to the romantic affair and there was, therefore, no need to establish the relationship. For example, after repeatedly asking Dayan whether his relationship with De Lima grew out of true love, a committee member asked, with a smirk, sarcastically and for no apparent reason but to grandstand and please his salivating colleagues, "So, ang sinasabi mo, ang relasyon mong ito kay Senator de Lima ay hindi lamang para saluhan siyang magtampisaw sa pagmamahalan o saluhan siya sa pagpawi ng init ng katawan?"

Another asked: "Sabay ba kayong matulog sa isang kwarto?" while still another asked: "Ano ang tawag nyo sa isa't isa" Another congressman, the same congressman who asked about the "init ng katawan" wondered: "Masasabi mo bang ang pagmamahalan ninyo ay tunay, matibay at wagas?" Each time these questions were asked and answered, the committee members and the gallery would break into malicious laughter.

The moral inquisition went for hours, obviously because it thrilled the committee members no end and gave them opportunity to grandstand and show that they were more macho than they looked. To the kanto boys drinking in the corner sari-sari store and the macho men used to talking about their sex exploits over cases of beer, it was a great "pulutan," as they would say.

The committee has presented several alleged witnesses, most of whom were convicted felons who stood to gain from cooperating with the Department of Justice and were afraid of going the way of Albuera, Leyte Mayor Ronald Espinosa who was killed inside his detention cell in an alleged shootout with members of the Criminal Investigation and Detection Group a few weeks ago that had all the signs of a rubout. The congressmen wouldn't even consider investigating the brazen killing, and yet would go all out to investigate and humiliate a sitting senator.

It should have been the words of scared convicted criminals against an elected senator and former DOJ and CHR chief. But the "honorable" congressmen would rather give more weight to the convicts' words despite the lack of any concrete evidence, such as paper trails and fat bank accounts!

Also, there were glaring inconsistencies in the testimonies of Kerwin Espinosa and Ronnie Dayan but the congressmen decided to ignore them and dwell on the romantic liaison between Dayan and De Lima.

What the seven-hour inquisition proved was that the House of Representatives that is supposed to represent the people in government policies is just a bunch of sexist, misogynist and indecent individuals who just happened to have the money to get elected to the House and get the title Honorable.

Then Inquirer columnist Manuel Quezon III first coined the term "Bastusang Pambansa" after the House lynched and unceremoniously ousted Speaker Jose de Venecia in 2008. The building that houses the House of Representatives is called "Batasang Pambansa" after the parliamentary body during the late years of martial law.

In 2009, bloggers and netizens again called the House the "Bastusang Pambansa" when the congressmen railroaded House Resolution 1109 in 2009 to allow Congress to reconstitute itself into a constitutional assembly (con-ass) to amend the Constitution and hopefully enable Gloria Macapagal Arroyo to either run for reelection or become prime minister.

After Thursday's hearing, the social media was abuzz again with the words "Bastusang Pambansa" to describe the inquisition. Rightfully deserved!

Ooooo

10
Massacre: 58 dead, 7 years, 0 justice
November 25, 2016

SEVEN years since 58 people, including 32 journalists, were slaughtered in what has been infamously called "Ampatuan Massacre" or "Maguindanao Massacre," not one of the 197 accused have been found guilty.

Four of the accused have since died, including the suspected mastermind, then Maguindanao Gov. Andal Ampatuan Sr. Of the 193 remaining accused, including 28 bearing the name Ampatuan, only 112 are in detention while 81 others have not ever been arrested at all! On the seventh year of the bloodiest election-related violence in the country and the worst attack on media men ever, the score remains lopsided in favor of injustice and impunity: 58 dead, 7 years, 0 justice.

Former President Benigno S. Aquino Jr. promised during the presidential campaign to prosecute those responsible for the brutal and brazen massacre, but the entire six years of his term passed without even a single man being convicted of the dastardly crime. And in all those six Aquino years and in the last months of the administration of Gloria Macapagal Arroyo, who was believed to be the benefactor of the Ampatuan clan of Maguindanao, several witnesses were gunned down and none of their killers have been arrested, much less convicted!

That means 81 of the massacre suspects are still out there, roaming around to possibly kill other prospective witnesses. With the current climate of impunity in the country, they can always kill those witnesses and have the bodies tagged with the cardboard that says they're drug pushers or users, and get away with more murders.

To remind us of what happened on that dark day, November 23, 2009, let me quote the narrative of party list Rep. Harry Roque, who was a lawyer for the family of one of the victims, in his privilege speech last Wednesday in the House of Representatives:

"Exactly seven years ago today, an entourage of 58 persons aboard a convoy of cars and vans were stopped by armed men at a police checkpoint in Karuan, Ampatuan, Maguindanao. They were then herded to a remote hill in Sitio Masalay a few kilometers away.

"When they reached the forlorn hill, the 58 captives met a gruesome death in the hands of a blood-thirsty band led by then Datu Unsay town mayor Andal Ampatuan Jr., scion and namesake of the state-backed local despot, Andal Ampatuan Sr., who, in his time, ruled Maguindanao with an iron fist.

"Of the 58 victims, 32 were journalists and media workers; the journalists and media workers joined the convoy to cover an entourage of women relatives of then Buluan town vice mayor Esmael Mangudadatu and led by his wife Genalyn.

"They were on their way to the Commission on Election's office in Shariff Aguak to file the vice mayor's certificate of candidacy for provincial governor.

"It was a grisly end for the convoy, put to a finis by the private army of strongman Andal Ampatuan Sr. whose son and namesake, "Datu Unsay" Andal Jr., was also vying for the post and did not want to see a rival to the post in Mangudadatu.

"Most of the victims were thrown into nearby pits earlier dug ostensibly for the purpose by a backhoe owned by the provincial government of Maguindanao. When police investigators finally reached the scene many hours later, they also found buried with some the victims in one of the pits a couple of cars from the ill-fated convoy.

"Apparently, there had not been enough time for the murderous band to bury everything — a few bullet-riddled vans belonging to the convoy still stood near the pits, their doors open, mute witnesses to a carnage that could only have happened because the Arroyo administration helped maintain and arm a warlord family for its own political convenience."

Year after year on the day of the massacre, November 23, journalists and relatives of the victims light candles in the hope that it would move the government to give priority to the resolution of the case and, therefore, show that amid the darkness, the light of justice would eventually prevail.

The Supreme Court reported last year that as of Nov. 23, 2015, the Quezon City Regional

Trial Court had "already heard a total of 178 witnesses (93 prosecution witnesses, 27 defense witnesses and 58 private complainants), which left us wondering how many more witnesses the court needed before it could make a decision.

Supreme Court spokesman Theodore Te also said the court was at that point wrapping up hearings on the bail petition of primary suspect Andal Ampatuan Jr. It took the court 5-1/2 years to hear the bail petition? By any standard of justice, that was really slow.

The International Freedom of Expression Exchange (Ifex), a Montreal-based network of 104 organizations campaigning for freedom of expression in 65 countries, said last year that the "glacial pace of the [legal] proceedings" of the massacre case was contributing to the "ingrained culture of impunity" in the country. Such a culture of impunity "not only denies justice to the victims of this [massacre] case" but also sows fear in society, hence "muzzles the media and promotes self-censorship," it added.

The reason that the culture of impunity continues is because nothing has been done to make the wheels of justice run faster. The culture of impunity will continue to cast a dark shadow over the country unless the government shows its resolve to arrest crime suspects and prosecute them to the fullest extent of the law and in the fastest time possible. Finding justice for the victims of the Maguindanao massacre would be a good start.

But the administration of President Rodrigo Duterte can't even show interest in investigating the extrajudicial killings of suspected drug users and pushers, how can it have the political will to resolve the Maguindanao Massacre? With the lead lawyer of the Ampatuan clan in the massacre trial, Salvador Panelo, having been appointed as presidential legal counsel, doubts have been raised as to whether the Maguindanao Massacre victims will finally get justice soon.

It's up to Duterte to prove critics and doubters wrong.

Ooooo

11
Gov't must probe brazen killing
November 11, 2016

THE KILLING of Albuera Mayor Rolando Espinosa was so brazen, and the excuse given by the police officers for the slaying so ridiculous, there is absolutely no reason for government authorities not to conduct a thorough and impartial investigation of the incident.

Why was Espinosa suddenly so brave and reckless to shoot at lawmen when just a few weeks earlier, he so feared for his life that he turned himself in to PNP Chief Director General Ronald de la Rosa on the first mention of his name in President Rodrigo Duterte's list of alleged narco-politicians? Espinosa could hardly be described as one who would be brave enough to shoot it out with policemen. In fact, he ratted his own son and associates to save his own skin and was reportedly willing to testify against personalities he had named as being linked to the illegal drug trade in his town.

Espinosa had named 226 persons as involved in the illegal drug trade, including politicians, members of the judiciary, CIDG and PDEA officials, and media members. Forty-seven of these persons have been criminally charged, including an aunt of the CIDG officer who led the assault on Baybay jail.

The mission of the men from the Criminal Investigation and Detection Group (CIDG) must have been so urgent and so important that they could not wait till morning to execute their alleged search warrant.

The CIDG men, according to the seven jail guards on duty at the Baybay jail at that time, ignored their demand to show them the warrant, herded them to once corner at gunpoint, and went directly to Espinosa's prison cell, where they were allegedly met with gunfire from Espinosa and another inmate from the adjacent cell, identified as one Raul Yap. Of course, the usual gun and packets of shabu were allegedly found in his cell.

However, the jail warden, Hormobono Bardillon, quoted his guards as saying that they heard Espinosa beg for his life.

"Ayaw gyud ko ninyo plantere, sir, wa ko armas nga gitago (Please do not plant evidence sir, I'm not hiding any firearms)," Espinosa was heard saying before gunshots rang out. Moments later, he and Yap lay dead. Did Yap really shoot it out with the policemen, too, or did he just have the misfortune of being at the wrong place at the wrong time, a possible witness to a murder that had to be eliminated, too?

Another factor that raised suspicions that the killing of Espinosa and Yap was a case of a rubout or an execution was that the closed circuit television footage that could have recorded the entire incident was conveniently missing.

Sen. Panfilo Lacson, who was himself alleged to have carried out summary executions during his stint as PNP chief, suspected as much that it was a clear case of extrajudicial killing.

Lacson believes Espinosa was silenced as he could name high-ranking PNP and government officials as protectors of illegal drug operations. "I have good information from my sources in Leyte that Kerwin (Espinosa's son who has been arrested in Dubai) and his father shared the same records of drug payola involving police officials and other police figures, the extent of which could reach very high level, both local and national," according to Lacson.

From the scant reports coming in based on statements from the jail warden and the guards, it would seem this is more of a rubout to silence a valuable witness against certain big-time drug lords and government officials, rather than an execution of a suspected drug dealer or user by law enforcers as has happened in the majority of the more than 4,000 already killed in Duterte's drug war.

Lacson noted that the killing of Espinosa came a few weeks after his lawyer and aide were killed. "Mayor Espinosa's alleged firefight with the local CIDG raiding team cannot simply be ignored as unrelated and coincidental," he said. He advised Sen. Dick Gordon to reopen the Senate's in vestigation into the extrajudicial killings.

Espinosa was the second town mayor named in the narco-list to have been killed under questionable circumstances. Mayor Samsudin Dimaukom of Datu Saudi Ampatuan, Maguindanao was killed along with nine of his companions in an alleged shootout with policemen manning a checkpoint in North Cotabato.

Police said Dimaukom's three-car convoy stopped just before reaching the checkpoint, and started firing at the policemen. While they were supposed to have been the first to open fire, not one policeman was killed and all in the mayor's convoy were shot dead.

The Senate should follow Lacson's advice and reopen its investigation into the extrajudicial killings. A crack team of investigators from the National Bureau of Investigation should also be able to ferret out which of the killings were the results of legitimate shootouts with policemen, which were rub-outs carried out by hired gunmen or policemen, which ones were summary executions carried out by law enforcers, and which ones were murders not related to drugs.

The government's continued inaction on these extrajudicial killings could be interpreted as a condonation of these violent acts or as a state policy. These daily killings could spiral into a culture of violence, and worse, a culture of death that could defeat any reform agenda that the Duterte administration has been implementing.

What's the use, for example, of having peace with the Muslim rebels and the communist insurgents, if there is no peace and order in the streets? How can there be peace when dead bodies surface nearly every day, not in the hills or in the jungles but on city streets – and now even inside the country's jails?

Ooooo

12
Agriculture is one bright spot
November 8, 2016

ONE bright spot in the Duterte administration is its giving attention to the resurgence of the agricultural sector as an important component of economic development. President Duterte, in his first State-of-the-Nation Address (SONA), said his administration would give priority to the optimization of agriculture production.

To prove his sincerity and determination to boost agricultural production in the country, the former Davao City mayor appointed as agriculture secretary former newsman Manny Pinol, who has extensive experience both as a farmer and as a provincial executive.

The President again showed this seal when he announced that he would revive the successful Masagana 99 and Biyayang Dagat programs that were implemented during the time of President Ferdinand Marcos.

Under the Masagana 99 program, the Marcos administration gave farmers nationwide access to improved technology, credit, price support for rice and provision of low-cost fertilizer. Masagana means bountiful while 99 was for the target yield of 99 cavans of rice per hectare per season.

It was launched in 1973 and in a few years, the country reversed a trend of importing rice to fill domestic needs, and in 1977 and 1978 was even able to export rice to other countries.

The Biyayang Dagat program, on the other hand, made available to fishermen nationwide liberal credit through thousands of rural banks all over the country to finance acquisition of fishing paraphernalia, diversified fishing activities, pay hired labor, and helped them improve marketing mechanisms.

Pinol reported during a meeting with Filipino community members in Toronto last week that during their trip to Cagayan to give emergency assistance to victims of the recent super typhoon Lawin, Duterte announced the turnover of not just relief goods but, more importantly, millions of pesos worth of rice and free corn and vegetable seeds to help the families recover.

Pinol said that even before he took over as agriculture secretary in July, he had been traveling across the country to meet with farmers and fishermen to determine their needs and to identify the crops that are suitable for certain areas.

Under the Duterte administration's "Back to Basics" approach to agricultural development, 10 steps are to be undertaken to ensure that Filipinos have enough food on the table and that agricultural and marine production are optimized to contribute substantially to the national economy.

Among these are determining the kind of food items that the market needs and quantifying the volume food that the Filipino people would consume every year, identifying which regions or provinces of the country would be suitable in the production of the needed food items, providing free irrigation services and basic infrastructures to facilitate the transport of food and agricultural products from the key production areas to the market, establishment of food terminals complete with cold storage facilities in key production areas, processing of food products at the local level, and providing support to fishermen to capitalize on the country's potential as a top producer of aqua and marine products given the fact that it is a country which has the fifth longest coastline in the world.

In the past administrations since Marcos' exit, agriculture has been relegated to the background despite the fact that the Philippines has always been an agricultural country for centuries.

For example. despite his boast that the country would be exporting rice in the second year of his administration, President Benigno S. Aquino III completely neglected the agriculture industry and, in fact, the opposite was true during his term: the Philippines imported even more rice and rice smugglers had a heyday that their activities virtually killed the local rice industry.

The administration of Gloria Macapagal Arroyo, on other hand, prostituted the agriculture industry by launching numerous programs where billions of pesos in government funds went to the pockets of politicians instead of to the intended beneficiaries – the farmers and fishermen.

Among these were the P720-million fertilizer fund, the P3.1-billion irrigation project, the P5-billion swine program, the P120-M Gintong Masagana Ani (GMA) program, and the P455-million ice-making machine program for fishermen. For some reason, the release of the funds for all these projects was timed a few months before the elections in 2004, 2007 and 2010. None of these programs were ever implemented and yet billions of the people's money were released.

Pinol blames corruption for the sad state of Philippine agriculture and assured that no such corruption would happen in his department. He pointed out, for example, that he refused to release funds for a contract signed into by the previous administration for the purchase of goats at what he described as exorbitant price. "I'm a goat raiser myself and I know that the price stipulated in the contract was way too much," he said.

Duterte and Pinol are right. The country needs to go back to the basics. Agriculture can provide the answer to spreading economic development to the provinces, which, in turn, will help decongest the urban centers. A successful agrarian reform program, with the government providing full support to the farmer beneficiaries, can help boost countryside development, and consequently, national economic recovery.

But first, corruption must be curbed. If the billions of pesos allotted to agriculture in the previous administrations were spent for the purpose for which they were intended, there is no reason the Philippines would lag behind its Asian neighbors in agriculture.

Duterte should give as much focus to agriculture and other economic issues as he does to his drug war and foreign policy. That would certainly do the country good.

Ooooo

13
From one master to another?
October 25, 2016

FROM one colonial master to another. From the frying pan into the fire.

This in essence is what breaking up ties with longtime ally United States and making friends with China, as announced by President Duterte, means. Getting out of dependence from one colonial master and getting into dependence with another does not make an independent foreign policy.

"With that, in this venue, your honors, I announce my separation from the United States, both in military ... not in social ... both in military [and] economics," Duterte arrogantly declares in a speech in China. "I have separated from them. So I will be dependent on you for all time. But do not worry. We will also help as you help us."

In. unequivocal terms, Duterte said he is breaking off virtually all ties with the US and will henceforth be dependent on China. Notice that the President also categorically used the word I, not the Philippines, which added confusion to the already vague foreign policy of his administration.

So, let's be clear on this. Does this mean all that he said was his own personal position? But as President, isn't he the sole source of the country's foreign policy and that all his statements can be construed as part of the country's foreign policy?

Based on his remarks, Duterte plans to go all the way in aligning the Philippines with China and eventually Russia, both communist and totalitarian states. Birds of the same feather flock together?

"I've realigned myself in your ideological flow and maybe I will also go to Russia to talk to (President Vladimir) Putin and tell him that there are three of us against the world—China, Philippines and Russia. It's the only way," he said.

In very clear terms, Duterte said he is realigning himself in communist ideology and, with his usual persecution complex, declares it's the Philippines, China and Russia against the world, as singer Helen Reddy would sing: "You and me against the world."

By realigning with the two communist nations, is Duterte abandoning long-revered democratic ideals, respect for human rights and the rule of law?

"The declared shift in foreign policy casting aside a longtime reliable ally to hastily embrace an aggressive neighbor that vehemently rejects international law is both unwise and incomprehensible," former Foreign Secretary Del Rosario said. "We must be with responsible nations with whom we share our core values of democracy, respect for human rights and the rule of law. To stand otherwise, is not what Filipinos are; it is not what we do; it is not what is right."

Even as president, has Duterte the right to drag the whole country, the entire 100 plus million Filipinos into such an ideology or into an uncertain future with an overly aggressive and ambitious China? As the leader of his people, doesn't the democratic way demand that he first consult with the people, including those who did not elect him, before making an unbelievable 180-degree turn in foreign policy?

Even Defense Secretary Delfin Lorenzana had to admit before a Senate committee that the President does not consult his Cabinet before making public pronouncements. Obviously, this is the reason Cabinet members and presidential spokesmen often grope for explanation whenever Duterte explodes one of his many bombshells. In the end, we all end up asking: What is it really?

Two days after saying in no uncertain terms that he was breaking up with the US economically and militarily, Duterte was saying he has no plans of severing ties with the longtime ally. What is it really?

"It is naive to think that a single person, even if he were president, can turn this foreign policy either way more than 45 degrees. Even the President's Cabinet hear, but don't accept, what this Rip Van Winkle of a President declares," Ateneo's Segundo Romero said, comparing Duterte to the main character in an 1800s American short story who falls asleep in the woods and awakes 20 years later to find the world around him changed.

Foreign Affairs Secretary Roberto Romulo, who was the country's chief diplomat under President Fidel Ramos in the 1990s, said Duterte should explain his move to the more than 60 percent of Filipinos who favor the US over China, and suggested that the President call a referendum before taking the country further down this path. "Past ambassadors to China warn not to trust China," he added.

Sen. Ralph Recto said of Duterte's Beijing remarks: "Any drastic shift in our foreign policy direction should be well-thought-out and not simply blurted out. It should be a product of deep study and wide discussion. Because of its far-reaching implications, it cannot be an announce-now, study-later thing. Crafting an independent foreign policy requires introspection, not impetuousness. This is all the more true if the object of the President's pique is not a backwater failed state, but a nation that is home to the largest number of Filipinos abroad, the biggest source of foreign exchange remittances, one of the biggest ODA donors, a major market of our products and services, like the BPO."

While we give credit to Duterte for being the first Filipino president to stand up to mighty America, we must also warn that he should be careful in threading that path.

"Relating with China must not mean surrendering our claim to the West Philippine Sea. Relating with China must not also mean accepting new neoliberal dictates through entering the Regional Comprehensive Economic Partnership (RCEP), which is essentially a China-led free trade agreement," said Kabataan partylist Rep. Sarah Jane Elago, who seems more mature than most of our current leaders.

One question that crops up immediately amid Duterte's nationalist rhetoric is why does he have to ask the permission of China to allow Filipino fishermen to fish in the rich fishing grounds of Panatag or Scarborough Shoal when it is clearly within the 200-mile Exclusive Economic Zone and that the UN tribunal has ruled that it is Philippine territory? He stands up against the Americans and bows before the Chinese? Is that what makes for his independent foreign policy?

Acting on his personal ideological prejudices and experiences with Americans, Duterte is dragging the Filipino people down a path that is full of uncertainties. For a nation that is still burdened by nagging problems of poverty, corruption, insurgency and political stability, uncertainty is the least Filipinos need at this time.

Ooooo

14
Cuddling up to China: Remember Scarborough
October 15, 2016

IT WAS bound to happen. Some very close allies of President Duterte are beginning to see through the perils of his administration setting its sights solely on its war on drugs, and cursing every person or entity that criticizes it, even to the extent of breaking off long standing ties with foreign allies and of sending the wrong signals to businessmen and investors.

Former President Fidel V. Ramos, who was among those who prodded Duterte to run for President, now expresses disillusionment in the first 100 days of the former Davao mayor's presidency. "In the overall assessment by this writer, we find our Team Philippines losing in the first 100 days of Du30's administration—and losing badly. This is a huge disappointment and letdown to many of us," said Ramos last Sunday in his column in the Manila Bulletin.

Ramos said "Team Philippines" was losing badly as the government focuses on the war on drugs at the expense of issues such as poverty, living costs, foreign investments, and jobs.

The former leader said Duterte could have hit the ground running "instead of being stuck in unending controversies about extra-judicial killings or drug suspects and in his ability at using cuss-words and insults instead of civilized language."

Duterte obviously won on a promise to feed the drug addicts and pushers to the fish in Manila Bay because it gave the voters an image of a strong ruler hell bent on crushing crime. But the President has to realize that the campaign is over and that there is no need to continue with his dramatics and that it is time to look at the broader picture.

Ramos said it correctly, that Duterte's war on drugs should not be the end-all and be-all of his governance and that the administration has to have a long-term strategic vision for the country.

Some of his other allies have urged Duterte to "mind his mouth."

In the House of Representatives, Majority Leader Rodolfo Fariñas advised Duterte "not to speak anymore" until he could adjust to refinement required of statesmen. In the Senate, Sen. Richard J. Gordon said Duterte has a duty to be a statesman and should moderate his language to protect the country against fallout from his outbursts over international criticisms against his brutal war on drugs.

To such criticisms, Duterte retorted: "Never mind my mouth. I never aspired to be a statesman."

At this stage of his presidency, Duterte should have realized that he is no longer the tough-talking mayor of Davao City, and is now the leader of a nation of more than 100 million people whose lives now depend on how he steers the ship. He cannot stay arrogant and unmindful of the general interest of the people, not just those of his own and of the 16 million who elected him.

In his dogged determination to defeat the drug menace, Duterte is losing sight of the fact that in the end, it will all boil down to the economy and how it will minimize poverty, which after all is the root cause of the drug problem and perhaps a litany of other problems that confront the country.

For example, because of his incessant attacks on the United States and European Union and his threats to break off ties with them, American and European investors, especially in manufacturing and business process outsourcing (BPO) are reportedly holding off on their investments.

In the month of June, after Duterte had been proclaimed president and started blasting people who criticized the killings that had been occurring at an alarming pace even before his inauguration as president, net foreign direct investments (FDI) recorded a steep drop of 40.9 percent.

For weeks now, the peso's value has been dropping vis-à-vis the dollar and the stock market continues to be in the losing column.

But Duterte remains unperturbed and says he would turn to China and Russia for trade and investments. The President even accelerated his rhetoric against the Americans, saying he would stop joint patrols between the US and the Philippines in the South China Sea, that the recent joint military exercise with the Americans was the last, that the country does not need military and other aid from the US or EU, and that "eventually, in my time, I will break up with America."

Duterte also called the US an unreliable ally, saying Filipino forces have not benefitted from the joint military exercises. Obviously still stung by the US' continued criticism of his human rights policy, Duterte retorted: "Instead of helping us, the first to criticize is this State Department, so you can go to hell, Mr. Obama, you can go to hell." Then addressing the EU, he said: "Better choose purgatory, hell is filled up."

Ramos and Supreme Court Justice Antonio Carpio scored the Duterte administration's anti-American foreign and military policy and urged President Rodrigo Duterte to stand for real independence and defend the country's territorial integrity.

Ramos said Duterte must learn to reach beyond his personal biases and think of his duties as being a responsibility to future Filipino generations. "I hope he shows more leadership in our lives. Not only in drugs," he said.

Carpio, on the other hand, urged Duterte not to discard the country's traditional allies because only one country can help the country in dealing with the West Philippine Sea issue. "There is only one power on earth that can stop the Chinese from poaching in our EEZ. That is the US," he said.

Later this month, Duterte will go on a state visit to China, which is expected to take advantage of the Philippine President's obvious ideological bias against the Americans and make many promises.

As he cuddles up to China, Duterte must not forget China's treachery during the Scarborough Shoal standoff in 2012 when after a US-brokered agreement to mutually withdraw from the shoal after a 10-week standoff, the Philippines withdrew its ships but China kept its patrol boats.

China has continued to occupy the Scarborough Shoal to this day, keeping Philippine fishermen from its rich fishing grounds, which are well within the 200-mile Exclusive Economic Zone. How can he trust a country that has shown treachery in the past?

Ooooo

15
Aquino, Abad must answer for DAP acts
October 9, 2016

STRIPPED of immunity and entitlements, former President Benigno S. Aquino III and former Budget Secretary Florencio Abad Jr. have finally been criminally charged for their roles in the notorious Disbursement Acceleration Program (DAP) which the Supreme Court had declared as unconstitutional and illegal in 2014.

Ten militant groups charged Aquino and Abad with technical malversation of public funds, usurpation of legislative powers, violation of the Anti-Graft and Corrupt Practices Act, grave misconduct, conduct prejudicial to the best interest of service and gross dishonesty.

The Supreme Court had ruled in July 2014 in a 13-0 vote that parts of the DAP were unconstitutional and the acts made out of the DAP program were illegal. The high tribunal even recommended that those responsible for these acts be prosecuted.

Despite the high tribunal's directive "to investigate and accordingly prosecute all government officials and/or private individuals for possible criminal offenses related to the irregular, improper and/or unlawful disbursement/utilization of all funds under the Pork Barrel System," not a single soul, particularly Abad, were subjected to investigation or prosecution by the Department of Justice.

Aquino could not be charged at that time because he enjoyed presidential immunity nor could he be impeached because of the overwhelming majority of the administration coalition in the House of Representatives.

Abad, on the other hand, remained untouched because of Malacanang's protection and this apparently emboldened the former budget secretary because even after the Supreme Court had ruled that his acts under the DAP were illegal, Abad continued to include in the 2015 national budget billions of pesos in un-programmed funds.

Either Abad had no respect for the law or the Supreme Court decision, or the need to create lump sums for the 2016 elections was so dire that he was willing to risk admonition from the court.

Abad tried to save himself from possible prosecution and to allow him and his Malacanang colleagues to continue their illegal DAP program by asking Congress to pass a bill he had submitted that sought to redefine "savings" and make the law retroactive.

In a letter to House Speaker Feliciano Belmonte Jr., Abad asked Congress to adopt and prioritize the draft bill that would effectively redefine the practice of impounding savings that the SC ruled as illegal and unconstitutional. He even requested Belmonte to consider the bill a priority measure.

With the redefinition of savings, the DBM had hoped that unspent funds for programmed projects even in the middle of the year could be pooled as savings, contrary to the SC ruling. Fortunately, the bill did not pass.

Aquino and Abad said the DAP was created in "good faith" but a statement in a bill filed by then Senator Aquino in 2008, Senate Bill 3121 entitled "The Budget Impoundment Control Act" showed that he had knowledge of the unconstitutionality and illegality of converting funds into "savings" in mid-year or realigning them outside of the congressional appropriations law, as they did under the DAP.

These were his exact words in the explanatory note of the proposed law:

"Clearly... while it is the President who proposes the national budget, it is the Congress that prescribes the form, content and manner of budget preparation albeit subject to the limitations found in the Constitution. Hence, as the 'power of the sword' belongs to the President, the 'power of the purse' resides in Congress."

"While its constitutional conferment is not expressed, the Administrative Code has given the President specific authority, when in his judgment the public interest requires and upon due notice to the head of office concerned, to suspend or otherwise stop further expenditure of funds allotted for any agency."

"Of recent times however, this presidential prerogative has been misused and abused, and has emasculated Congress' authority to check the President's discretionary power to spend public funds. In effect, the President seems to have a vast and unbridled control over the national budget."

"What Aquino denounced then as immoral, abuse and misuse of powers, Aquino was also doing now in the case of the illegal DAP," former Bayan Muna party list Rep. Nilo Colmenares said then. "President Aquino from the start knew that the DAP was illegal."

Using DAP funds, Malacanang released from P50 million to P100 million to each senators a few weeks after the Senate voted 20-3 to convict Chief Justice Renato Corona in his impeachment trial in 2012.

Was it just coincidental that the three senators who voted against conviction — Senators Bongbong Marcos, the late Miriam Santiago and Joker Arroyo – did not get a single centavo from the DAP? Or perhaps the three didn't have urgent projects that merited an 'accelerated disbursement"?

At that time, the militants vowed to file criminal charges against Aquino and Abad once they left Malacanang, and last July 8, the groups, led by the Volunteers Against Crime and Corruption (VACC) and Bagong Alyansang Makabayan (Bayan), trooped to the Office of the Ombudsman and filed a 26-page complaint against the two former officials.

"The DAP was nothing more than presidential pork taken from forced savings then realigned for pet projects of the President," Zarate said. "It was not a stimulus program as many of the projects approved by Aquino had nothing to do with stimulating the economy."

The ball is now in the hands of Ombudsman Conchita Carpio Morales, the former Supreme Court justice who swore Aquino into office in 2010 and who was appointed by Aquino to her present position. Let's hope she has not been bitten by the "selective justice" bug that was prevalent under the Aquino administration.

Ooooo

16
Same-sex marriages in PH?

October 6, 2016

IT IS about time that a discussion on the possibility of legalizing same-sex marriage is started in the Philippines. That the initiative came from House Speaker Pantaleon Alvarez, who has shown the same tough guy image as his friend President Duterte, is surprising, but is definitely welcome news.

In the United States, although same-sex marriage has been legalized federally, the controversy continues over unions between two persons belonging to the same sex. Some states, like North Carolina where voters approved in 2012 an amendment to the state constitution affirming that marriage may only be a union between a man and a woman.

The debate over same-sex marriage first stirred the world and Americans' consciousness in 1993 when the Hawaii Supreme Court ruled that denying licenses to same-sex partners violated the Hawaii constitution unless there was a "compelling state interest." In 2004, Massachusetts became the first state to legalize same-sex marriage. Six states immediately followed in allowing gay marriages: Connecticut, Iowa, Massachusetts, New Hampshire, New York, and Vermont, plus Washington, D.C. and Oregon's Coquille and Washington state's Suquamish Indian tribes.

Worldwide, a few countries have begun to allow same-sex couples to marry, the first of which were Argentina, Belgium, Canada, Iceland, the Netherlands, Norway, Portugal, Spain, South Africa and Sweden.

I didn't see the Philippines catching up on gay rights in the near future. In fact, Alvarez's proposal met instant opposition from several congressmen. But that it is being discussed and a proposed bill waiting submission in the House are good signs that the country is finally catching up on gay rights. Another good sign is the appointment of gay couple Aiza Seguera and Lisa Dino to government posts.

The country has remained centuries behind in its cultural and religious beliefs because of the stranglehold of the Roman Catholic Church. In fact, then President Aquino, through spokesman Edwin Lacierda categorically stated that his administration was not ready to accept the concept of gay marriage. Then Speaker Sonny Belmonte also said the House of Representatives was not keen on passing a law that would allow same-sex marriage. They would rather allow ignorance, inequality and bigotry to prevail over the country than offend the Church.

In November 2008, while America was upholding the result of decades of battle for civil rights by electing Obama, an African American, to the presidency, tens of thousands of Californians were institutionalizing inequality, injustice and bigotry by passing Proposition 8, which sought to ban gay marriages in California. They wanted to include in the state constitution a provision that would deprive a group of people of their right to happiness and equal protection, and on the same breath would rather protect the rights of chickens, pigs and cows than those of their fellow human beings.

Californians voted 52% to 47% to pass Proposition 8. Sixty-three (63) percent of these same Californians voted to mandate proper handling of farm animals through Proposition 2.

Proposition 8 sought to include in the state constitution the words: "Only marriage between a man and a woman is valid or recognized in California."

The framers of the constitution of both the state and the United States of America, included the protection of individual rights precisely to ensure that such rights could not be taken away by legislative or administrative action, or even by the "tyranny of the majority."

In a ruling that revoked an earlier proposition to ban gay marriage, the California Supreme Court correctly pointed out that the right to marry is one such constitutional right that must be provided equally to all people desiring to marry.

Those who oppose gay marriages claim that the union of same-sex couples undermines the "traditional" definition of marriage and thus poses a threat to the institution of marriage. In March 2005, US Judge Richard Kramer noted that a violation of individual rights could not be justified by its historic acceptance. It must also be pointed out that more than 18,000 same sex marriages have been legalized in the US for years, but the "traditional" institution of marriage has not been put in peril, nor has society collapsed. Nor have these marriages degrade the marriage of traditional man-woman couples.

The legalization of gay marriages does not require those who have moral objection to them, to recognize or approve of these marriages. Neither does it require priests or church ministers to perform or bless such marriages. Neither does it require schools, as falsely claimed by gay marriage opponents, to teach that there is "no difference" between the traditional man-woman marriages and same-sex marriages.

Many proponents cite the Bible saying that the Holy Scriptures describes marriage as that between a man and a woman. These religious fundamentalists tend to forget that gays are God's creation, too, so why treat them differently? Why deprive them of their right to be happy, to spend their life with the person they love, and experience the joys of having a family while enjoying the benefits and protection of the law? Can they honestly say that God feels differently about gays?

Many gay couples have been together for 20, 30, even 40 years, far longer than many traditional marriages. As correctly pointed out by the San Jose Mercury News in an editorial: "All couples who exchange vows know, in their own hearts, the depth and spiritual meaning of their union. That is for them, not others, to determine."

I say, amen.

Ooooo

17

Playing both sides won't do it

October 1, 2016

N THE first few days of his presidency, President Duterte gained favorable response from the business community after his announcements that he would give emphasis to infrastructure development and making transactions easy for businessmen. With just a few hundreds killed in Duterte's drug war, they were willing to look the other way.

But as the death toll from the brutal drug war breached 1,000 and the administration started labelling politicians and businessmen as drug lords or accomplices without solid evidence, those from the business community began being concerned about the government's regard for the rule of law. And while the end objective of the drug war is to bring back peace and order, investors are getting worried that the culture of violence that the drug war has cultivated and the disregard for the rule of law might eventually affect how they live and conduct business in the country.

This concern or fear, if you may, plus the uncertainties in both domestic and foreign policies are beginning to show its toll on the country's economy.

Last week, data from the Philippine Stock Exchange showed net foreign transactions on the benchmark index have fallen over the past month. A CNBC report said, "Many investors have been turned off by threatening remarks made by Duterte against the US and China, casting doubt on the future of Manila's foreign policies and his handling of the economy."

The Economist, on the other hand, said that since Duterte took office, investors have demanded higher risk premiums to hold Philippine assets. "A lot of people are hesitant to put their money into the Philippines at this point," according to Guenter Taus, who heads the European Chamber of Commerce in the Philippines.

After Duterte tagged business mogul Roberto Ongpin as an oligarch he wanted to destroy, and Ongpin was forced to resign after the shares of his company fell 50%, the fear among businessmen and investors was raised another level.

Recently, Standard and Poor expressed concern that the Duterte administration's campaign against illegal drugs might hurt local economic growth. The credit reporting agency also said the Philippines is unlikely to get a credit rating upgrade in the next two years due to Duterte's unpredictability in domestic and foreign policies.

And how did Duterte react to all these?

The tough-talking President said investors are free to leave the country; he's not a believer of the stock market anyway. Duterte said foreign businessmen who cannot stand his foul mouth could pack up and leave the country if they want. Duterte said he could always go to other allies such as China and Russia to seek trade and investments for the country.

He used the China and Russia cards again. As he continues to hint at bearing away from longtime and reliable ally the United States, Duterte in the past few weeks have said that he would seek new alliances with China and Russia to cushion the fallout from possible withdrawal by the US.

On Tuesday, Duterte said he had "crossed the Rubicon" in his ties with the US and that he would pursue partnerships with its rival countries or what he called countries on the "other side of the ideological barrier." In a speech on Tuesday at the Navy headquarters, Duterte asked the Marines to give him time so "we can get out of this ambit" of the Americans "who have pushed us around, insulted us." On Monday, he announced his plan to meet Chinese President Xi Jinping and Russian Prime Minister Dmitry Medvedev after flying to Vietnam and Japan. He also said the country plans to purchase arms from Russia.

He also said in the past few days, in quick succession, that the US Special Forces should leave Mindanao, that the Philippines would no longer conduct joint patrols with the US in the South China Sea, and that the last joint US-Philippine military exercises would be the last.

And yet, earlier, the President said the Philippines needs the US for the South China Sea, where it remains locked in a territorial dispute with China. Foreign Secretary Perfecto Yasay Jr. again went on clarifying mode as he said the President has no plans of cutting ties with the US and that the "crossing the Rubicon" remark was just his dramatics aimed at bolstering relations with US rivals China and Russia.

Yasay slipped. It would appear that Duterte is trying to play the US on one side and Russia and China on the other in an effort to gain benefits from both sides. For example, he has been sending signals to China that he would welcome financial assistance for his railway projects and to Russia for cheaper weapons. But by playing both sides – just as he is playing both the communist rebels and the military, wooing both of them with promises – Duterte may be playing with fire and may be putting himself in a position where he could antagonize both sides in the long term.

Also, this has caused a perception of uncertainty in both his domestic and foreign policies. Where is he really taking the country? Does he want the country to be a socialist state that is allied with communist powers Russia and China? Or does he want the country to remain a democracy with strong ties to longtime ally US? Duterte seems inclined to the first, but the people, I'm sure, favor the second.

Perhaps, Duterte wants the country somewhere in between, enjoying the benefits of sleeping with both sides. But then, we all know that considering the strategic location and importance of the Philippines to this part of the world, this is just not possible. It could burn him, and scorch the entire country with him.

Duterte's dramatics and derring-do may be good for his popularity ratings in the short-term, but these will eventually have adverse effects on the economy as local and foreign investors begin to wonder if it's worth staying in the country under a cloud of uncertainty.

While 16 million Filipinos voted for Duterte mostly on his promise of eradicating drug addiction and other crimes, and gave him a 91-percent approval rating in July, those numbers could dwindle and disappear fast if he fails to improve the economy and bring food and job to the people. Threatening a longtime ally and cavorting with its enemies certainly won't make it happen.

Ooooo

18
Never again: Just another slogan?
September 25, 2016

MANY Americans are up in arms again after two more apparently unarmed black men were shot down by policemen. Protests in Charlotte, North Carolina have turned violent and North Carolina Governor Pat McCrory had to declare a state of emergency after a protester was shot and a policeman was injured on the second night of protests.

Earlier in Tulsa, Oklahoma, another unarmed black man was shot dead by the police and protests have also mounted. For several months now, protests have mounted all over the United States over police killings of mostly black men, which have triggered the Black Lives Matter movement. Every single police-involved shooting have been met with violent protests, from Baton Rouge, Louisiana to St. Paul, Minnesota.

The United States is a bastion of freedom and democracy and Americans value human rights, due process and the rule of law. That's why even a single incident that shows disrespect for human rights and disregard for due process and the rule of law is met with massive protests.

In the Philippines, more than 3,000 suspected drug dealers and users have been gunned down in cold blood both by police and vigilantes and just a few howls of protest have been heard. Instead, the daily murders have been met with cheers and approval, with the murderers offered words of praise and the perpetrators given high approval ratings for their "achievement."

Angered by the proliferation of illegal drugs and the increasing number of young people addicted to them, many Filipinos are willing to turn a blind eye on the disregard for due process, the rule of law and perhaps, even their hard-fought freedom in the name of peace and order, if you can call the current state of lawless violence, culture of impunity, and of lifeless bodies left daily on the streets a peaceful and orderly society.

Emboldened by the seeming public approval and nonchalance, presidential legal counsel Salvador Panelo, whose clients include Ampatuan massacre accused Mayor Andal Ampatuan Jr. and double murder accused Calauan Mayor Antonio Sanchez, among others, is now tinkering with the possibility of granting President Duterte extraordinary powers through a "constitutional dictatorship."

Such a dictatorship, Panelo says, would give his boss power over both the executive and legislative branches of government, exactly the same powers that the late President Ferdinand Marcos had for the duration of martial law, during which time the late strongman abolished Congress and exercised sole legislative functions through presidential decrees.

And Panelo says it's all constitutional, in other words not a mockery of the constitution because, he said, the charter would be amended to give the President the expanded powers. How can you argue with that kind of thinking? So, if murder is illegal, just amend the Revised Penal Code and scrap it from the list of punishable crimes and it becomes perfectly legal. No wonder the Philippine justice system is in disarray because many lawyers think like Panelo.

Even during the presidential campaign, Duterte had shown a strong dislike for Congress and a tendency towards strongman rule. He threatened to abolish Congress if elected president if it blocks his reform agenda. Prior to his swearing in, he basically threatened media when he declared that corrupt media men are open to assassination.

In late April just a few days before the elections, in a visit to an NPA camp to facilitate the release of five policemen held hostage by the communist rebels, Duterte said he plans to install a revolutionary government because, he said, Congress can no longer address the country's problems. He said he would "revolt from the inside," which reminds us of Marcos' own calls for a revolution from within prior to suspending the writ of habeas corpus and declaring martial law.

Duterte has also shown he cannot handle criticisms and a dislike for any kind of opposition. Duterte goes ballistic each time he is criticized, especially with regards to possible human rights violations. He explodes into expletives when questioned about the extrajudicial killings, calling even the likes of respectable world leaders US President Barack Obama and UN Secretary General Ban Kim-moon "son of a b…," "stupid," "moron," "fool," among many other "colorful" words.

When Chief Justice Lourdes Sereno bewailed the disregard for due process and the rule of law in the killing of drug users and pushers, Duterte threatened to declare martial law if the Supreme Court intervenes.

Duterte has shown his vindictiveness. I thought former President Noynoy Aquino was the most vindictive Philippine president ever when he personally destroyed Supreme Court Chief Justice Renato Corona and moved mountains, using people's money through the illegal Priority Development Assistance Fund (PDAF), to impeach Corona whose only crime is his alleged misdeclaration of his Statement of Assets, Liability and Net Worth (SALN) and, of course, his leading the Supreme Court in handing a decision against the Hacienda Luisita owned by the Cojuangcos and the Aquinos.

But Duterte's own vendetta against Sen. Leila de Lima, who had investigated the Davao Death Squad when she was chairman of the Commission on Human Rights, for speaking out against the extrajudicial killings and the nation being caught in a "slippery slope to tyranny," is cruel and brutal.

To her credit, De Lima continues to fight back, although her only weapon, the chairmanship of the Senate committee on justice, has now been taken from her coincidentally after she had produced Edgar Matobato, a self-confessed executioner under the DDS who was delivering a bombshell that could warrant murder charges against Duterte if he were not protected by presidential immunity.

Amid all these, the opposition, or what's left of it, remains relatively silent. The Liberal Party, which has joined the administration coalition in both houses of Congress, has been accused of plotting to oust the President despite their willingness to cooperate with his administration. Except for a meek rallying behind their beleaguered party mate De Lima, the Liberals are not using their superior number in both the Senate and the House to protect her and to stand for their party.

This administration has either become too paranoid or is up to something.

Communications Secretary Martin Andanar last week revealed an alleged plot being hatched by some Filipino-Americans in New York to oust Duterte, although he was quick to admit that it was just mentioned to him by somebody who was in the meeting. In other words, hearsay. Why a high-ranking government official would reveal an unverified information that could cause concern among businessmen and the people is beyond me.

There appears to be coordinated efforts to make the country look unstable. Duterte, for example, said during a speech in a military camp that we should expect another bombing in Mindanao.

Also, Duterte has been visiting military camps in the past few weeks. In each stop, he promises the soldiers higher pay, more benefits and better weapons, as Marcos did decades ago. He also said last week that he plans to revive the Philippine Constabulary, which would make the police part of the Armed Forces of the Philippines again, a move obviously aimed at consolidating his control over both the police and the military.

These moves remind us of what Duterte told Rappler in October last year of his plans for a revolutionary government, as reported by veteran investigative journalist Raissa Robles: "It's going to be a dictatorship. It's the police and the military who will be the backbone. If they agree with you – if the right thinking policemen and military men agree with you – then after six years, there will be a new set-up: maybe a federal type, less corruption, and a fresh air for the next generation."

But this week, Duterte assured the people there will be no martial law. Didn't Marcos say that, too, when he suspended the writ of habeas corpus, and a few months later, declared martial law?

Last Wednesday, the nation remembered how Marcos declared martial law 44 years ago, and in so many ways, as the people have repeatedly said since the People Power on EDSA ousted the dictator, proclaimed: "Never again." And yet, most of them watch by as the country slowly slips into tyranny.

Ooooo

19
DepEd should focus on science
September 25, 2016

AMID all the negativity created by the daily murder of suspected drug dealers and users, the numerous foreign policy gaffes, the claims and counter-claims involving President Duterte and Senator Leila de Lima, and moves by certain quarters to turn the President into a "constitutional dictator," is a piece of good news coming from the Department of Education that assures us that it has begun to realize the need to push science education in the Philippines.

On Friday, Education Secretary Leonor Briones said the Department of Education is hiring more math and science teachers to boost science education under the K-12 program.

When the K-12 program, which added two extra years to basic education, was launched in the 2012-13 school year, some sectors were concerned that the Education department was dropping the teaching of science in the early grades, and would instead focus on developing the students' English language skills to prepare them for an expected boom in business process outsourcing (BPO) or what we know as the call center industry.

There was reason to be concerned if indeed the K-12 program would focus on developing the Filipino students' English language skills, instead of their scientific and analytical skills.

But this wasn't the case because late in 2011, the Department of Education announced that it had added 100 more schools to the 100 schools that offer specialized curriculum focused on Science in its effort to train more scientists.

Then Education Secretary Armin Luistro said the 100 new special science elementary schools (SSES) consist of Special Education Centers (SPED) with programs for the gifted and talented child and selected regular schools that passed the SSES screening procedures.

SSES was designed to develop Filipino children with scientific and technological knowledge and skills plus creative and positive values that will make them catalysts in spurring research and development thrusts. It provides enriched curriculum for Mathematics and Science where gifted and talented learners are provided a venue and exposure to develop their aptitude and skills.

The need to focus on math and the sciences has become even more urgent in the wake of a report in 2009 by the United Nations Educational, Scientific and Cultural Organization (UNESCO) that the Philippines is lagging behind in the scientist-population ratio when compared to other countries.

The report said there were only 125 scientists and engineers per million people engaged in research and development in the Philippines. The UNSECO average for developing nation is 380 scientists and engineers per million population.

In 2008, there was a study that showed that the Philippines was in the bottom of 38 countries tested in the efficiency of their math and science education. The test was conducted among eighth grade students of the 38 countries (second year high school equivalent in the Philippines) to see how effective the current math and science education programs in these countries were.

The Philippines placed well below the bottom in both the math and science categories, beaten even by Thailand and Malaysia.

That same year, Sen. Edgardo J. Angara lamented that the Philippines was in the bottom third of the global competitiveness list of 117 countries, and he attributed this laggard status to the Filipinos' general failure to keep up with the advancement in science and technology throughout the world.

It would be a big mistake for the Philippines to shift its focus from math and science to developing the students' English language skills just to make the country more competitive in the BPO business. In fact, it would be a tragic mistake for the government to rely on the BPO industry for economic development just as it would be a mistake for the country to depend on the remittances of overseas Filipinos for long-term economic growth.

Both the BPO and remittance sectors depend on outside factors that are not under the control of the country. For example, there are moves in Washington to discourage the outsourcing of jobs by US companies. With the current economic problems being experienced by

European countries, they can follow the example of the United States and try to bring back jobs in their own countries, thereby crippling the BPO industry in the Philippines.

While remittances from overseas Filipinos continue to grow, there is always the danger that the hiring countries would no longer depend on foreign workers once their own citizens being to develop their own skills, or would have to do away with foreign labor when their own economies are at a downturn. In the US, for example, which has tightened the door to new immigrants, a new generation of Filipino-Americans who would have no attachments to their homeland will arise, thus greatly reducing remittances to the Philippines.

Look at India and China. While they are the leading BPO providers in the world and two of the biggest remittance recipients, they continue to give serious attention to the teaching of math and science, which has led to their leadership in the computer industry and in the manufacturing sector. These two countries, which also are among the top countries in the math and science tests mentioned in the article, are producing the most number of highly paid computer experts and executives in Silicon Valley and in other computer capitals.

These two countries have also produced the finest doctors, medical researchers and engineers in the United States. It is no wonder that both China and India are among the richest countries in the world, and their economies are growing at a pace faster than any of the traditional industrialized countries, such as the United States and Germany.

The Philippines enjoys one of the highest literacy rates in the world. But the students' literacy are not directed towards careers that will eventually bring growth and wealth to the country, such as in computers, engineering, agriculture, and scientific research. Instead, Philippine colleges and universities continue to produce mostly graduates in business and the arts.

The Philippine educational system is not designed to meet the demand for technological skills. A study by the Department of Labor and Employment in 2011 showed that firms engaged in science and technology would generate 4 millions jobs in the next five years, but educational institutions can produce only 2.7 million graduates in these fields during that period.

The educational system could give the Philippines a competitive edge if it focuses on math, science, technology and engineering.

For example, education officials should lure back Filipino students to the prestigious International Rice Research Institute, which has produced great agriculture scientists for Thailand, Taiwan and Vietnam but not for the Philippines. Thus, Thailand, Taiwan and Vietnam are raking in billions of dollars in agriculture while the Philippines, which has perhaps the best and most number of agricultural colleges, continues to lag behind.

Ultimately, it is agriculture and the manufacturing sector that will bring long-term positive effects on the country's economy, and not the short-term BPO and remittance sectors.

We hope that under Secretary Briones, the government would redirect the Filipino students' energy and enthusiasm in education to math, science, engineering and computer sciences, and feel the impact of growth in the years to come.

Ooooo

20
Even in foreign policy, people matter
September 16, 2016

I'M pretty sure Foreign Secretary Perfecto Yasay Jr. has been having some sleepless nights since he assumed office in July. He has the unenviable position of having to explain and clarify most of President Duterte's remarks involving foreign policy, specifically those pertaining to the Philippines' longtime ally United States. And they're not few.

Yasay had to rush to Washington D.C. last week to try to soothe the hurt feelings and the deep concerns that Duterte has inflicted on the world's most powerful country and the Philippines' most dependable ally for decades.

Specifically, Yasay is seeking a meeting with US State Secretary John Kerry in an apparent attempt to mend fences with Washington after Duterte called for US troop withdrawal in Mindanao. Yasay said he would assure Kerry that there is no change in the country's foreign policy. Malacanang itself has stated that the President has not issued an official statement on the matter.

On Monday, Duterte said he wanted US forces out of Mindanao and blamed America for the restiveness of Muslim militants in the region. It was the first time he publicly opposed the presence of American troops in the country although he had stated many times, in various ways, that he has no love for Americans.

Duterte has had an uneasy relationship with the US since assuming the presidency in June and has been openly critical of American security policies. As a candidate, he declared he would chart a foreign policy that would not depend on America.

The President's uneasy ties with the US gained its crescendo when before leaving for the Asean summit in Laos, he used expletives as he blasted US President Barack Obama when asked by a reporter how he would respond if Obama raised the issue of human rights. While Duterte expressed regrets for the remarks, for which he blamed media's quoting him out of context, the President went on to verbally attack American atrocities during the US pacification campaign in Mindanao a century ago in his speech before the Asean leaders.

Upon his return, the unrepentant Duterte said again that he did not like the Americans and said the 100 or so American Special Forces troops in Mindanao should leave the country.

This was later followed by another remark that the Philippines is considering buying weapons from Russia and China. Again, Yasay and Duterte's defenders in Malacanang had to clarify the statement.

Duterte's obvious ideological prejudices against the United States, obviously a hangover from his Kabataang Makabayan days with Communist Party of the Philippines founder Jose Maria Sison are exacerbated by his constant pronouncements that he was ready to engage in bilateral talks with China despite the country's recent legal victory in its territorial dispute with China in the UN Permanent Court on Arbitration.

Duterte said he was expecting plenty of help from China, an apparent follow-up to his musing after he was proclaimed the winner of the May 10 presidential elections that he would sit down with China if it would help fund the Philippines' railway project.

The President may be repeating the same mistake that Gloria Macapagal Arroyo made when she struck a deal for the joint exploration of the South China Sea apparently in exchange for the controversial NBN-ZTE broadband deal that was eventually dropped amid corruption allegations. This emboldened China to be more aggressive in the South China Sea.

Duterte is obviously looking at China in terms of how the economic giant can help the country economically, particularly in terms of trade and infrastructure development. But former Economic Planning Secretary and NEDA Director General Cielito F. Habito, who served during the time of President Fidel V. Ramos, debunked myths that an economic partnership with China is more important to the Philippines than with the US.

Habito said the US is more important to the Philippines as an export market, accounting for 15 percent of our total exports in value terms, against China's 10.9 percent. As source of imports, the reverse is true, with official figures showing less of the country's imports (10.8 percent) coming from the United States than from China (16.2 percent).

"Offhand, it appears that proportionately more workers benefit from our exports to the United States than to China, with labor-intensive manufactures more prominent in our top five exports to the former," Habito said.

He added that as source of foreign direct investments, the US is far more important to the Philippines than China, accounting for 13 percent of total net FDI inflows in 2015, against China's negligible 0.01 percent (less than $1 million).

As for remittances, Habito said, Bangko Sentral ng Pilipinas data report that nearly half (43 percent) comes from the United States, and less than 1 percent from China. "It would seem from all this that on purely economic terms, we stand to lose more from antagonizing the Americans than the Chinese," he said.

From an economic standpoint, however, it would be wise for Duterte to keep the country's ties with both countries on even keel. The United States remains the world's biggest economic power with China coming closely at second.

Duterte, however, has to be careful in issuing statements or making reckless remarks on foreign policy, especially on matters that would alter the balance of power in Asia. By sending wrong signals regarding its relationships with either US or China, Duterte is playing into the hands of China, which is obviously hoping to divide the Asean countries as it moves to grab military superiority in the region.

Coming as it does during America's pivot to Asia, Duterte's tirades against the United States and the softening of the country's stand against Chinese aggression in the South China Sea could have a critical impact on the balance of power in the region.

The Philippines is at the forefront of the battle against Chinese aggression in the South China Sea and holds an ace in having won a very important legal battle on the sea dispute. As in the game of poker, it would be unwise for the country to fold when it holds an ace in his hand.

As Duterte has repeatedly said, he is now the president of the Philippines and not just the mayor of Davao City. As such, he represents the voice, the hope and aspirations of the Filipino people. He can no longer speak based just on his own ideological prejudices, but must reflect the interest of the people. Does he believe that the 16 million people who voted for him resoundingly want the country to favor China over the United States? How about the other 90 million or so Filipinos, who also look to him now as their leader?

Ooooo

21
Did he really say that?
September 13, 2016

DID President Duterte really say he wants American Special Forces to leave Mindanao and that he purposely did not attend the meeting between the leaders of the Association of Southeast Nations because he did not like the Americans? Or was it another one of those reckless utterances that would be denied or clarified later by his spokesmen and Cabinet members?

In the case of his recent remark that he intentionally did not attend the Asean leaders' meeting with Obama as a matter of principle because he did not like the Americans, it was the reverse, with Duterte making a liar of his spokesman in Malacanang who had issued an official statement saying that the President was not in the meeting because he fell ill.

But in most instances, Presidential Communications Secretary Martin Andanar, Presidential Spokesperson Ernesto Abella, Presidential Legal Adviser Salvador Panelo, Agriculture Secretary Manny Pinol, Foreign Affairs Secretary Perfecto Yasay Jr. and other close advisers had to scramble for ways to clarify statements that Duterte had made before media men and during his speeches.

These series of clarifications and denials started just after he had been declared the winner of the May 10 presidential elections. When asked about media killings during a press conference in Davao city, Duterte blurted out expletives and justified the murder of some media men, blaming corruption in the media and irresponsible reporting for the slayings.

"It's not because you're a journalist you're exempted from assassination if you're a son of a bitch," he added. Duterte said the freedom of expression enshrined in the 1987 Constitution would not protect reporters from assassination if they are corrupt or careless in reporting.

When told that the international media group Reporters Without Borders is calling for a boycott of his press conferences, Duterte blurted: "I was saying, you idiots, do not threaten me. I said I'm ready to lose the presidency, my honor or my life. Just do not fuck with me."

Panelo said Duterte's statement on the killings of journalists was "taken out of context, misinterpreted and misunderstood."

Senator Aquilino "Koko" Pimentel III, president of Duterte's party PDP-Laban, on the other hand, appealed to the public not to "misinterpret" Duterte's statement. "Ang sinabi lang naman ng Presidente, we have freedom of the press but we also have to be responsible in exercising it and given the nature of the Filipinos, sometimes they resort to violence and the Constitution can't protect you from violence."

"We need a little understanding. He does not have any bad intention," Vitaliano Aguirre II, Duterte's justice secretary, said. Aguirre II, Duterte's designated justice secretary, said. "He uses hyperbole to attract attention to what he wants to say... He intentionally exaggerates, like during the campaign. You have to give him some leeway… so his statements can be interpreted so that it could be toned down."

After this incident, Duterte finally decided to listen to his advisers and kept his silence until his inauguration and his first State-of-the-Nation Address in July. And then he got a 91-percent popularity rating in the surveys and the real Duterte resurfaced.

There are many instances when Duterte delivered expletives against international figures, such as Pope Francis, the American and British ambassadors, United Nations Secretary General Ban Ki Moon, and two UN special rapporteurs, among others. But his gaffe with US President Barack Obama takes the cake.

When asked by a reporter how he would respond if Obama asked him about human rights concerns in his deadly drug war, Duterte said: "I do not have any master except the Filipino people, nobody but nobody. You must be respectful. Do not just throw questions. Putang ina, I will swear at you in that forum."

Malacanang immediately issued a statement, saying: "He (President Duterte) regrets that his remarks to the press have caused much controversy. He expressed his deep regard and affinity for President Obama and for the enduring partnership between our nations."

Panelo, on the other hand, accused the US government of "misreading" Duterte's comments. "Don't put meaning to that. That's just his style. It's just a hyperbole. It's just an expression. I don't think it was directed to President Obama," he said, which was echoed by

Agriculture Secretary Manny Pinol and Senator Alan   Cayetano.
It was too late. The White House had cancelled the bilateral meeting between Obama and Duterte.

And then, in an obvious attempt to save face, Malacanang said Duterte would be seated between Obama and UN's Ban during the state dinner for Asean leaders. It turned out Duterte was seated several seats from both Obama and Ban.

The public relations problem is confounded by the fact that there are just too many eager beavers among his close aides who rush to his defense whenever Duterte makes an earth-shaking remark, adding to the confusion.

Before he left for Laos, Duterte declared a state of lawless violence following the Davao market blast that killed 14 and wounded several others. Presidential Management Staff head Christopher Go said the declaration was only for Mindanao, but Panelo and Abella later said the order would cover the entire country.

Panelo, for unexplained reason, later clarified that the Davao blast did not trigger the declaration because it had been planned for some time and that, in fact, a draft has been made and that it was scheduled to be announced on Sept. 4 or 5, which was a day after the Davao bombing.

In another speech last week, Duterte said the source of the list of police generals linked to the illegal drug trade was given to him by former President Fidel V. Ramos, who obviously complained about the revelation, prompting

Presidential Adviser on the Peace Process Jesus Dureza, a longtime Ramos aide, to say the reports were pure "fabrication." This despite the fact that Duterte clearly stated it in his taped speech.

And then on Monday, Obama said he did not like Americans that's why he did not attend the meeting with Obama in Laos and that he wanted the US Special Forces out of Mindanao. "For as long as we stay with America, we will never have peace in that land," Duterte said.

He again showed black-and-white pictures of what he described as Muslim Filipinos, including children and women, who were slain by US forces in the early 1900s and dumped in a pit, with American soldiers standing around the mass grave in Bud Daho, a mountainous region in southern Sulu province.

If he did say that, is he in effect making a complete turnaround in the country's foreign policy, which for decades has treated America as an ally, and, in fact, has made the US a treaty ally? Is he giving us a hint that the Philippines, under his watch, is ready to sever this decades-old ties, and scrap all the treaties that are in effect, including the Mutual Defense Treaty and the Enhanced Defense Cooperation Agreement (EDCA)? Is he preparing to embrace China and Russia, two communist states, as evidenced by his proudly proclaiming that he had one-on-one meetings with Russian President Vladimir Putin and Chinese Premier Li Keqiang while saying he purposely snubbed Obama?

As President, Duterte should know that every word that comes out of his mouth about other countries and leaders could be interpreted as a shift in, or declaration of foreign policy. He has been consistent in declaring that he has no love for America even during the campaign and has blamed the longtime ally for some of the country's miseries. Is this a sign of a major foreign policy shift?

Or are these remarks to be regretted again later, with his platoon of spinners and defenders again coming out with confusing clarifications?

Ooooo

22
PH can't stay in middle for long
September 9, 2016

LESS THAN two months after the Permanent Court of Arbitration in the Netherlands overwhelmingly ruled in favor of the Philippines against China in their territorial dispute over portions of the South China Sea, President Duterte refused to capitalize on this legal leverage by not discussing the ruling during the recent summit of the Association of Southeast Asian Nations (Asean) in Vientianne, Laos.

Instead, he focused on his campaign against illegal drugs as he tried to rally the Asean leaders behind his brutal drug war that has already killed more than 2,000 suspected drug pushers and users, and which has earned condemnation from all over the world.

With the UN tribunal ruling, which in unequivocal terms validated the country's sovereign rights over that part of the sea it calls the West Philippine Sea, the Philippines should have rallied the Asean to issue a stern warning against China for its over-aggressive expansionist activities in the disputed sea.

As a result, China won its second straight diplomatic victory in the Asean Summit when the regional grouping issued a joint statement that cpouildn't be called a "mild rebuke" because the Asean couldn't even get all of its 10 members to agree that China was responsible for building islands in the disputed and resource-rich sea.

A statement issued at the end of the Asean summit said in regard to the South China Sea, "We remain seriously concerned over recent and ongoing developments," without elaborating and without even mentioning China by name.

The statement said the summit "took note of the concerns expressed by some leaders on the land reclamations and escalation of activities in the area, which have eroded trust and confidence, increased tensions and may undermine peace, security and stability in the region."

The statement did not even mention the UN tribunal ruling.

And yet, the day before he left for Laos, Duterte had complained that Chinese ships and barges were spotted near Scarborough Shoal in a clear proof that despite the UN Tribunal ruling, China continues to conduct reclamation activities in the shoal, which is well within the Philippines' 200-mile Exclusive Economic Zone.

Duterte even directed the Department of Foreign Affairs to summon the Chinese ambassador to explain the construction activities. During a Cabinet cluster meeting in Malacanang, Duterte was reported to have remarked: "Why is China treating us this way? Is it because we are a small country which does not have the capability of standing up to them militarily?" Still, Duterte refused to follow up on his complaint nor even bring up the matter of the UN tribunal ruling and the sea dispute during the summit discussions.

More than two months into his administration, Duterte continues to send mixed signals on the country's territorial dispute with China.

During the campaign and in one of his early press conferences, Duterte said he was ready to enter into bilateral talks with China on their conflicting claims over several islets and shoals in the South China Sea.

In February, he said he was open to bilateral negotiations with China over the possibility of joint exploration of the Spratlys, echoing Beijing's line. He also said he might be willing to soften the Philippines' stance significantly — if China would build railroads in Bicol and in Mindanao. "Build us a railway just like the one you built in Africa, and let's set aside disagreements for a while," he said.

Duterte was also skeptic about the Philippines' case at the tribunal, saying the ruling wouldn't be worth anything if China didn't comply with it. "I have a similar position as China's. I don't believe in solving the conflict through an international tribunal," he said.

In April, he said he was ready to die to assert the country's claims over the disputed islands in the South China Sea but on the same breath, he said he would go to China and talk to its government if the latter refuses to comply with the decision of a UN arbitration tribunal hearing the Philippines' case against China.

By constantly saying that the Philippines is leaning towards holding bilateral talks, the government is dissipating the advantage it has gained through the victory in the tribunal.

As Duterte shows vacillation in his China stand, Beijing has been emboldened to continue its military buildup in the region through its artificial islands. As early as June, US patrols have observed Chinese vessels surveying the disputed Scarborough Shoal (Panatag Shoal) for another possible reclamation project. This was confirmed by the Philippine military last week and by Filipino fishermen early this week.

Scarborough Shoal is just 120 nautical miles off the coast of Zambales and just 200 nautical miles from Manila. It is around 470 nautical miles from the closest point on the Chinese mainland.

In April, US Defense Secretary Ashton Carter had said the US is concerned about possible reclamation by China in Scarborough Shoal, citing a potential risk of military conflict.

"We take that seriously, very seriously," Carter told a congressional session, mentioning the view that China could begin reclamation work later this year at Scarborough Shoal, which has been seized by China despite an ownership claim by the Philippines.

"It's a piece of disputed territory that, like other disputes in that region, has the potential to lead to military conflict," Carter said.

Duterte has to make clear his stand this early before tensions in the area, which has been considered one of the hottest flashpoints in the world, explode into a direct military conflict between the US and China. He wouldn't want to be caught in the middle or on the wrong side when that happens.

Ooooo

23
No need for emergency declaration
September 7, 2016

WE CHEERED President Duterte when he ordered the military to pursue the Abu Sayyaf after the group of bandits beheaded an 18-year-old hostage two weeks ago following the failure of his family to come up with the P1-million ransom.

After all, Duterte had said in July that the Abu Sayyafs were not criminals and that they resorted to violence only because of desperation brought about by the failed promises to them by the government. I found Duterte's remark illogical because he considered the small-time drug users and pushers "not humans" and worth killing without due process, ignoring the fact that more than the Abus, most of those killed in his brutal drug war were driven into desperation by their poverty, which, in turn was the result of the failure of their national leaders.

But just as soon, he changed his tune and said they were indeed criminals, after they brutally beheaded their hostages whose family or government refused their demand to pay the ransom. And when the Abus beheaded the helpless 18-year-old and heartlessly informed his family of the beheading, Duterte ordered 10,000 troops to pursue the bandits.

An all-out war against these bandits have long been overdue, but here was Duterte, finally realizing that just as he has committed the full resources of the national police to the war against drugs, he has to employ the full force of the military to eliminate this other scourge of Philippine society.

And then he had to declare a state of lawlessness, or lawless violence, or national emergency, or whatever you want to call it. Was it necessary?

Duterte and his officials were quick to defend the state of national emergency declaration, which empowers the President to call on the military to help the police suppress and prevent violence. But he had already called on the military to help the police to fight both the drug dealers and the Abu Sayyaf without resorting to a state of lawless violence declaration, why declare it anyway?

Duterte's supporters said it was necessary following the bombing attack on Davao's night market, which killed 14 and injured around 70 of Duterte's constituents in Davao City. But Presidential Legal Adviser Salvador Panelo said the Davao blast did not trigger the state of lawless violence declaration and that it had, in fact, been planned long before the Davao blast. Panelo also said that Executive Secretary Salvador Medialdea had made a final draft that was scheduled to be announced on Sept. 4 or Sept. 5, which coincidentally was a day after the Davao blast.

If it was not triggered by the Davao blast, what was then the basis for the declaration of a state of lawlessness? Unless they are admitting that the spurt of drug-related killings has caused a state of lawlessness and a culture of violence throughout the country.

Panelo said the reasons for the declaration were the ongoing campaign against illegal drugs, criminality, terrorism and the offensive against the Abu Sayyaf. He said the police alone cannot do the job and it is therefore necessary to call on the Armed Forces to assist the Philippine National Police.

It cannot be helped that many people were concerned about the declaration, having had a bad experience with similar attempts to use extra powers purportedly to suppress lawlessness and violence in the past.

Although the most telling of these bad experiences happened more than 40 years ago, Filipinos still cannot forget that the late dictator Ferdinand Marcos used the same excuse when he suspended the writ of habeas corpus in 1971 after the bombing of the Liberal Party rally in Plaza Miranda. Many student leaders and activists were jailed without arrest warrants.

Marcos lifted the suspension less than five months later, only to declare martial law on September 21, 1972 for basically the same reason, with the alleged ambush of then Defense Secretary Juan Ponce Enrile as the trigger. Opposition leaders, foremost of which was then Sen. Benigno Aquino Jr., media members, student leaders and activists were incarcerated. Newspaper offices, radio and TV stations were closed. Freedom of the press and speech were suppressed. It took nine years before Marcos lifted martial law, but he continued to rule until he was deposed in the 1986 People Power Revolution.

And more recently, Gloria Macapagal Arroyo declared a "state of lawless violence" in 2006 and ordered the military and police to prevent and suppress acts of terrorism and lawless violence in the country. She claimed there was an attempt by communist rebels and rival politicians to unseat and assassinate her.

In the one week that the declaration of national emergency was in effect, police arrested Anakpawis Rep. Crispin Beltran, Bayan Muna Rep. Josel Virador, newspaper columnist and UP Professor Randy David and Akbayan president Ronald Llamas. Police also raided the opposition papers Daily Tribune, Malaya and Abante.

Although Duterte and his spokesmen assure that the declaration of national emergency is not a prelude to martial law or the suspension of the writ of habeas corpus, it is sending a chilling effect on the administration's critics and on the media. "What if he declares martial law?" is a question that now lingers on the minds of those who would dare criticize him. What if some members of the police and the military misunderstand their newfound powers and abuse them? What if Duterte, who is not great at taking criticisms, suddenly decide to arrest critics and close down media outlets?

These are valid concerns based on the people's previous experiences with similar adventures on emergency powers.

"When you declare a state of lawlessness, this could lead to abuses on political, civil and human rights in the implementation of the declaration, like what happened when former president Gloria Macapagal-Arroyo declared a state of lawlessness, and it spawned unwarranted illegal arrests, which the Supreme Court no less debunked as illegal," Lagman said.

And that's precisely why the recent declaration of national emergency should be lifted the soonest possible time and not allowed to run its 60-day limit allowed by the Constitution.

Ooooo

24
Why I Publish/Reprint Books

Tatay Jobo Elizes
Self-Publisher

Writings are timeless and they act as mirrors to history. I publish writings as they remain relevant anytime. I have seen a lot of good writings in the internet, in magazines and newspapers. But most writers have only one or two articles and therefore not enough material to be published as a book. And yet, many of them need to be published or archived. There are also writers who write a lot but never publish them. There are also old books with no more prints available. The solution is to publish/reprint.

I do this for free because of the print-books-on-demand (POD) system, but the printed or hardcopy is not free

The printed book will always be there among your collections or libraries. Not all use the internet. The internet access has its technical problems. I can produce fiction, non-fiction, in color also.

My booklist can be seen at http://tinyurl.com/mj76ccq (copy and paste)

Permission had been granted by the author/authors to print their books under my free self-publishing service. They own copyrights to their works.

Interested reader may request free reading of any of my books, articles or essays via online reading or ebook. Just select and email me.

Thank you.

ooooo